The Inteꞏ
Challengꞏ

Cormac Lankford

BLACKHALL
Publishing

BLACKHALL PUBLISHING
26 Eustace Street
Dublin 2
Ireland

e-mail: blackhall@tinet.ie

© Cormac Lankford, 1999

ISBN: 1 901657 41 8

A catalogue record for this book is available from the British Library.

Printed in Ireland by
Betaprint Ltd

Contents

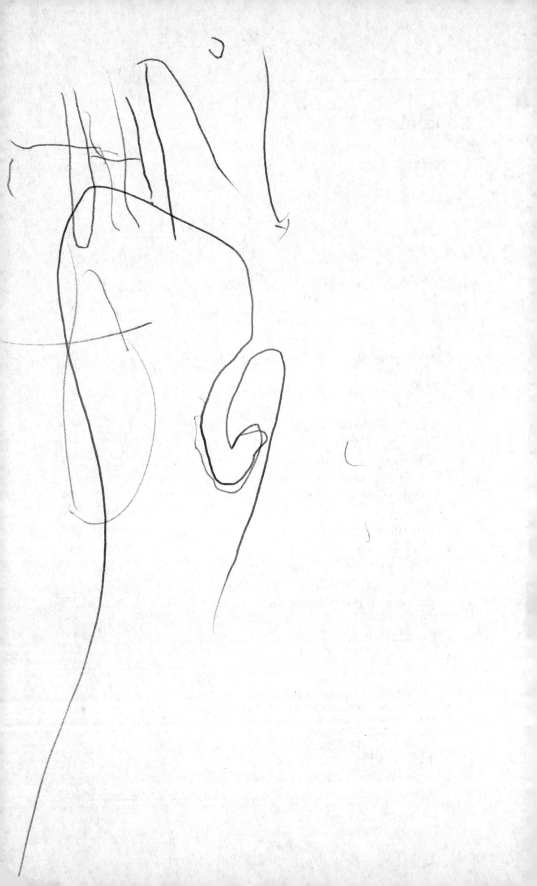

Preface

The idea for this book arose from a thesis which the author submitted for a Master's Degree in Applied Psychology at University College Cork in 1989. The thesis examined the interview skills of hundreds of job applicants by asking practicing training managers, personnel managers and managing directors to evaluate the videotaped recordings of such interviewees in interview settings. The author also conducted a survey among approximately 60 multinational and indigenous companies in the south of Ireland.

Therefore, the comments of real interviewers and research, arising from recent studies conducted into interview procedures on banks, the army, the police and many other organisations, formed the background for this book. There is no better way of establishing what the requirements of interviewers are than by asking them to comment on the performances of interviewees. In this way, it is possible to identify the behaviour which employment interviewers regard as acceptable and the answers which the expect to receive. This is precisely what was done as preparatory work and it is within such a framework that the author developed the hard-headed, practical steps for success that are outlined here for job applicants. Furthermore, the select bibliography, given at the end of the book, clearly demonstrates how closely related to the needs of the real world the book is.

The employment interview cannot be described purely as a 'game' or as an exercise in 'communication skills', as some commentators would have us believe, nor can it be dealt with through reliance on certain sterile rules or precepts. For this reason, the reserach has been carefully sifted and the comments of company interviewers have been organised in such a way that the reader can find useful tips no matter which section of the book is opened. Special care has been taken to avoid complex sentences, which many worried interview applicants have little time to read through.

The author gives examples of actual interviews, answers, CVs, aptitude tests and selection policies that are taken from his research into the contemporary situation. It is suggested that you use these as models for your interview. You are asked to fill in a number of preparatory questionnaires and you are given sample tests to do, the answers for which are provided. These are kept to a minimum because the objective of the book is to reduce the amount of preparation that the busy job applicant has to do. While a degree of self-analysis is encouraged, the focus of the book is on the tangible and real task of coping with the interview.

The style of writing is direct, succint and user friendly, so that the candidate will be equipped to deal with the employment interview as a challenge which can be met head on, by proper planning, adequate rehearsal and thorough research. It is clear, from the unemployment statistics throughout Europe that it is only the most skilled people, in every sense, who will progress. This book will concentrate your attention on how you can translate your life experiences and skills into 'marketable assets' during your interview challenge.

Cormac Lankford
February 1999

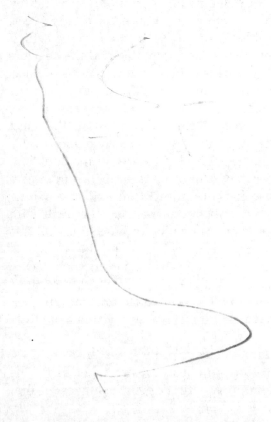

1

What The Interviewer Wants To Know

The list of characteristics under which interviewers rate candidates includes the following and they are frequently placed in the order of importance given below. Each one will be dealt with in this chapter.

> *Intelligence*
> *Education*
> *Knowledge of the organisation*
> *Confidence*
> *Communication skills*
> *Leadership*
> *Evidence of research*
> *Coping with stress*
> *Diction*
> *Appearance*

But what questions do interviewers ask in order to discover whether you are intelligent, communicative or articulate? How do they establish your level of education, your leadership qualities, knowledge of the world or your self confidence? How is the ability to cope with stress measured and how do you demonstrate evidence of research? Above all what can you do about your appearance? The following questions are a guide to the kinds of questions that interviewers might ask in order to establish the degree to which they consider applicants to be competent in the above characteristics.

Intelligence

Likely Questions	Poor Answers	Comments	Good Answers
Why did you choose your optional subjects at school?	I chose them because there weren't any others available.	Vague, suggests a lack of focus and direction.	I chose my subjects on the basis of my aptitudes and my career interests.
Did you drop any subjects and, if so, why?	Yes. I didn't like the subjects very much and I detested the teacher.	Gives a negative impression.	The subjects I dropped were not relevant to the career areas for which I was preparing.
In what way are the subjects you chose relevant for the job for which you are applying?	Economics gives you an idea about how the country works.	Rather incomplete.	Economics gives me a grasp of how factors, such as the law of diminishing returns can affect production on the shop floor in your company.
Could you mention an application of physics to the real world?	Physics is about the physical environment.	Incomplete.	In the real world physics is one of the subjects that gives an understanding of important ideas, such as speed, velocity, friction and many other physical happenings.
And chemistry?	Chemistry is useful for understanding the effects of pollution.	Incomplete.	Chemicals are used in the flavouring of commercially produced food, such as ice cream.

Communication Skills

Likely Questions	Poor Answers	Comments	Good Answers
How would you establish good rapport between yourself and a client or customer?	I would talk to him/her.	Says nothing.	I would try to talk about the client's field of interest.
How important is it to be able to relate to a client or customer?	Very important.	Too brief.	Without a good relationship with the customer or client no business can take place.
What makes you think that you would be capable of establishing good customer relations?	I like meeting people.	Non-committal and uninteresting.	From my involvement with football teams, committees and voluntary groups, I have acquired good communication skills.
How would you deal with difficult customers?	I would tell them that is the way the organisation does it and tell them to take their business elsewhere if they didn't agree.	"The customer is always right?"	The only way to deal with difficult customers is to agree with them while, at the same time, gently promoting your own interests and putting forward your own point of view.

Education

Likely Questions	Poor Answers	Comments	Good Answers
What were the leading stories in today's newspapers?	There were stories about politics and unemployment.	Says nothing.	The leading stories in today's newpapers dealt with pollution, unemployment and the introduction of breathalyser tests.
What improvements are required to the educational system?	There should be more practical subjects.	Superficial.	It is crucial that the educational system adjusts to the needs of modern society.
How well do you think the educational system prepared you for life?	It teaches you very little about the world of work.	Misses the point of the question.	The educational system gave me training in how to think logically and to evaluate constructively. These characteristics have given me confidence in myself.
Which subject do you think is the most relevant for this job?	Physics.	Too short and insufficient development.	The subject I found most relevant was philosophy because it taught me how to analyse topics in a rational way.

Likely Questions	Poor Answers	Comments	Good Answers
Which projects did you find the most useful?	The economics project.	Says nothing.	The project I found most useful was on food hygiene. Through it I learned how to gather, classify and present information in an interesting way.
How important are extra curricular activities at school?	They develop personality.	Shows poor communication.	Extra-curricular activities give a person a very positive attitude to life and develop efficient interpersonal skills.
In what way does poetry help you gain an understanding of yourself and life around you?	Poetry teaches you about culture.	Too general.	Poetry has made me sensitive to the needs of others.
In what ways do you think it is useful for students to study Shakespearean plays?	Shakespeare is the greatest English dramatist.	A rather barren response.	The universal concepts that are emphasised in Shakespearean plays are applicable in many real life situations in contemporary life. His advice not to be a borrower or a lender be is as appropriate today as it was in his time.

Leadership

Likely Questions	Poor Answers	Comments	Good Answers
What are the qualities of a good manager?	A good manager should be able to lead effectively.	Too short.	A good manager will have the capacity to listen, co-ordinate the insights of others and to act effectively.
What is the best way of motivating people?	By giving incentives.	Too vague.	The best way of motivating people is by delegating responsibility and giving 'ownership'.
How would you deal with a strike situation?	I would negotiate with the workers.	Shows a lack of understanding.	The most effective way to deal with strikes is to maintain dialogue between all factions so that common ground can be reached.
What skills did you learn in team games that would be useful to a manager or leader?	Team games teach you how to win.	Does not address the question.	Participation in team games teaches potential leaders and managers to work as an integral part of a group because the good of the individual has to be subordinated to the group.
What positions of leadership did you hold?	I liked being in charge.	This answer avoids the issue.	I was class prefect, secretary of a society, scout leader, team captain and a school debater.

Likely Questions	Poor Answers	Comments	Good Answers
In what way would you say a manager is the first among equals?	The manager is the leader of the group.	This answer is not detailed enough.	A manager is the first among equals insofar as his/her background is similar to those of the workers and the organisation's goals are shared by all.
To what extent do you think the development of initiative is useful?	Initiative helps people to get things done.	Does not say how.	Initiative is the driving power behind all human endeavour and without it organisations die.
In what way do you think the ownership of the company can be shared?	People can be given more responsibility.	Shows poor comprehension.	Ownership of the company can be shared by asking employees to formulate the goals of the organisation. You can then ask them to accept reponsibility for the achievement of these goals.
Could you explain how a project you have completed involved leadership skills?	I learned how to work on my own.	The basis of the question has been misunderstood.	I compiled a project at school in which I had to conduct research, gather data together and draw firm conclusions. This is the way good managers will find solutions to problems.
What is creative management?	Acting in a creative way.	Not a sufficient answer and too vague.	Creative management is the ability to respond to situations in an innovative way.

Knowledge of the Organisation and Evidence of Research

Likely Questions	Poor Answers	Comments	Good Answers
What do you know about company X?	Company X is a mulitnational company.	This is mere common knowledge.	Company X is a multinational company involved in the research, manufacture and marketing of health care products.
Could you name the products the company produces?	The company produces medicines and toothpaste.	No evidence of research.	The company's products include drinks X and Y, toiletries, shampoo, over the counter medicines and toothpaste.
What recent development has the company undertaken?	The company is researching new drugs for heart treatment.	Undeveloped answer.	The company is currently researching treatments for bacterial, viral and fungal infections.
Do you understand the company's approach to training?	Employees are trained on the job.	Too general and vague.	Employees are recruited for specific jobs rather than being put into training programmes. In this way they make an immediate contribution to the business.

Confidence and Coping with Stress

Likely Questions	Poor Answers	Comments	Good Answers
You don't really think that you have the character-istics for this job do you?	I suppose I haven't really.	Very negative.	Well, I feel that my track record speaks for itself. You can see from my CV that I have the knowledge, the background and the personal characteristics to succeed.
What job do you expect to hold in ten years time?	I would expect to be working in the same job.	Lacks ambition.	After gaining experience in the various sections of this job, I feel that I would have acquired the characteristics to be successful in a more senior position.
Could you give a brief account of the un-employment problem?	The problem with un-employment is very serious. The government should focus on reducing the number of unemployed people.	Demonstrates a superficial grasp of the subject.	The un-employment problem has become a per-vasive problem in all modern economies. One of the great anomalies of the present problem is that it appears to be quite prevalent where technology has created a lot of wealth.

Likely Questions	Poor Answers	Comments	Good Answers
Why should we choose you rather than one of the 500 other people who applied for a position at this theme park?	Because I can do the job well.	Doesn't reject the negative implications of the question.	You should choose me because I am a very capable worker as my track record and CV show. I know that I have more ability than many other applicants for this job.
If your supervisor asked you to handle a dangerous chemical, how would you react?	I would simply refuse.	Too curt.	I would say that I would rather not handle the chemical without consulting the safety officer first.
Your results in accounting are very poor aren't they?	I suppose that they are.	Concedes too much.	I intend to focus specifically on this subject in the future. Furthermore, I feel that my scores in other subjects, such as economics, will compensate for my accounting results to a certain extent.

Diction and Appearance

These two factors are not tested for directly but are assessed at all stages throughout an interview. It is felt that they give the interviewers vital clues to a person's general mode of expression. All facets of your expression need to be attended to. In other words you need to be conscious of your intonation, word stress and accent. It is largely through your speech peculiarities that you are going to sell yourself as an enthusiastic, well-adjusted and well-informed person.

Interviewers are constantly watching for tell-tale clues about your attitudes. Feelings of indignation, inadequacy, dissatisfaction and despair can easily be conveyed in oral communication. Look carefully at the sentence below and note how placing the stress on the words in bold can change the impression that is given.

*"I felt that they shouldn't have changed **me** to another job."*
(Indignation)

*"I felt that **they** shouldn't have changed me to another job."*
(Criticises employers)

*"I **felt** that they shouldn't have changed me to another job."*
(Indicates a certain arrogance)

*"I felt that they **shouldn't** have changed me to another job."*
(Criticises management's role)

All of the above responses may be perfectly acceptable in particular contexts. However, the interview candidate has to be careful not to display characteristics verbally that reveal him/her in an unfavourable light.

In general, it can be said that when you are expressing an opinion your tone of voice is not a major problem. When you are justifying a course of action you must be extremely careful to present a balanced viewpoint. Indignation, rejection, anger and criticism of others should be firmly controlled in case the interview panel begins to feel that you may acquire the same kinds of feeling in the job for which they are interviewing you. *Employers are not interested in taking on potentially difficult employees.*

Appearance cannot be judged very well through asking questions. At the same time, interviewees should be careful about questions which deal with their attitude to dress and appearance. In general, it can be said that interview panels do not like male applicants to have long hair or to wear earrings, black clothes, heavy boots or jeans when they are attending an interview. In regard to females, very short skirts, over use of cosmetics and extremely tight fitting clothes are generally taken by interview panels to indicate that the applicant may be more likely to be interested in how she looks herself rather than in the job for which she is applying. However, it is very difficult to draw conclusions about clothes, looks and general appearance.

KEY CONCEPTS

- Where appearance and dress are concerned take no chances.

- Your emotions and feelings are revealed in your mode of expression.

- Monitor your diction as the interview progresses in order to ensure the right impression.

- Beware of factors that symbolise non-conformity such as earrings, black clothes and longer or dyed hair.

- Open your mouth when you are speaking, never mumble your answer.

- Try to ensure that there is a smooth, even flow in your speech.

- Don't let the ends of sentences fall or trail away.

- Avoid very long sentences that could land you in trouble.

- Keep most of your answers in the form of statements.

- Keep your voice at the appropriate pitch for the space that exists between you and the interviewers.

- Avoid using too loud or domineering a tone of voice.

2

Getting To Know Yourself

If you want to impress the interviewer, or the interview panel, you need to demonstrate that your aptitudes and interests, as well as your knowledge, fit in well with the job for which you are applying.

Due to the fact that job opportunities are often in short supply, applicants have got to concentrate on those jobs for which they are equipped rather than on those for which they have no talents. Tips and guidelines for performing well in aptitude tests are given in Chapter 8. To gain knowledge of the job for which you are applying the specific research which you conduct into the area, will illustrate your level of interest and commitment in a most dramatic way.

Deciding What Area You Are Really Interested In

You have got to look at yourself first. The important thing for you to keep in mind, as you set out to impress others, is to be able to impress yourself. You have got to analyse your own interests. If there are discrepancies you have got to identify them and either change your interests or apply for a different career area. Therefore, you have got to discover what is your pattern of vocational interests.

There are 96 careers listed in Table 1 and they are divided into sections, from A to H. You should indicate your first career choice in each section and rate it as your number 1. Your second choice in each should be rated as number 2. Then, you continue indicating your career preferences, in this fashion, until you come to your least preferred career in each section which you rate as number 12. Then, total your preferences across the table so that you can identify the category totals and their ranks.

You must have a clear idea of what your career profile really

Table 1: Survey of Career Interests

Careers	List A	List B	List C	List D	List E	List F	List G	List H
Mechanical	Engineer	Tool Maker	Electrician	Mechanic	Telecom Engineer	Watchmaker	Radio Engineer	Welder
Computational	Accountant	Bookkeeper	Statistician	Tax Assessor	Maths Teacher	Cashier	Financial Controller	Accountant
Scientific	Meteorologist	Chemist	Biologist	Agricultural Scientist	Botanist	Astronomer	Geologist	Lab. Assistant
Persuasive	Sales Representative	Radio Announcer	Marketing Executive	Interviewer	Company Representative	Auctioneer	Public Relations Officer	Insurance Sales Person
Aesthetic	Commercial Artist	Interior Artist	Architect	Photographer	Stage Designer	Window Dresser	Textile Designer	Designer
Literary	Journalist	Novelist	Historian	Librarian	Magazine Reviewer	Book Reviewer	Script Writer	Poet
Musical	Pianist	Conductor	Music Critic	Music Teacher	Organist	Record Librarian	Band Leader	Music Shop Assistant
Social Service	Psychologist	Teacher	Social Worker	Religious Position	Policeman or Woman	Youth Worker	Employment Officer	Counsellor
Clerical	Bank Manager	Company Secretary	Private Secretary	Clerical Officer	Insurance Clerk	Office Worker	Postal Clerk	Town Clerk
Practical	Carpenter	Builder	Painter	Bricklayer	Wood Machinist	Plasterer	Plumber	Mason
Medical	Doctor	Veterinary Surgeon	Pharmacist	Dentist	Optician	X - Ray Therapist	Nurse	Physio-therapist
Outdoor	Farmer	Forester	Surveyor	Water Diviner	Gamekeeper	Fisherman	Truck Driver	Gardener

is. Try to have all thoughts focused on this profile for your interview. In this way you will impress with your conviction, your motivation and your 'feel' for the job in question. From each of the lists of occupations below fill in your rankings from 1 to 12. In order to demonstrate how this analysis works out in practice look at Table 2 below, which illustrates the type of profile accountants will have because their first choice is clerical, the second is computational and the third is persuasive.

Table 2: Career Interests Profile for an Accountant

Categories	Ratings	Rank
Mechanical	76	10
Computational	11	2
Scientific	80	12
Persuasive	37	3
Aesthetic	78	11
Literary	66	5
Musical	72	8
Social Service	73	9
Clerical	8	1
Practical	57	4
Medical	66	5
Outdoor	68	7

Now complete Table 3 by placing your results from Table 1 in the appropriate categories.

Table 3:   Personal Career Interests Profile

Categories	Total Ratings	Rank
Mechanical Computational Scientific Persuasive Aesthetic Literary Musical Social Service Clerical Practical Medical Outdoor		

According to researchers if your score for any of the above categories comes to less than 25, it demonstrates that you have a very strong preference for such a category. If no clear pattern emerges in your career interests it would really pay you to think well about what you are applying for. You should try to make your career interests, as consistent as possible, so that if you are asked questions about the kind of jobs that are closely related to the career area you are applying for, you will be well able to respond.

If your first, second or third choices fit in with the career area for which you are applying, you should be well on your way to persuading the interview panel that you are the right person for the job. However, if your first three choices are totally unrelated to the job you are applying for, you would want to be able to make sure that your replies do not contain tell-tale signs that you are unfit for the job. It should be added that this is also true of CVs and application forms. If your career choice pattern is not consistent with the position in question, perhaps you should rethink your choice of career.

Tips to Rectify Weaknesses in your Career Pattern and Interests

- Visit the local library, the reference section as well as the main lending section, for information on the employment situation.
- Examine an encyclopedia for career information that will develop your interests.
- Talk to people who have similar careers to those in which you are interested.
- Read the daily newspapers for articles about new companies.
- Contact the agencies that deal with industrial development to see what plans exist for future economic development.
- Note from the newspapers which companies and which sectors are expanding.
- Study the reports of Trade Union Congresses that deal with the career areas in which you are interested.
- Study the career profiles of people in the areas of interest so that you can adjust your own profile if necessary.
- Talk to people in the job, find out their interests, aptitudes and achievements.

Dejargonisation

Avoiding the use of language and terms which are not familiar or in every day use is what dejargonisation is all about. It is necessary for anyone working in a specialist field to use terms which everyone can understand, even when they are explaining some technical process. If they can communicate with the interviewer they can clarify what benefits they can bring to intending employers.

Engineering

It is particularly necessary for engineers to be able to dejargonise their language. Engineers spend long periods of study time at subjects such as mathematics, electronics and physics. They have very little opportunity of communicating what they have learned in a non-technical way. In many cases it may be lay people who will interview them. *They will need to be convinced that the candidate can operate effectively in a work environment.*

It is of little use for an engineer to have a highly developed understanding of the principles of hydraulics if he/she cannot transmit this knowledge in a simple way to a workforce. If you are an engineer and an interviewer asks you the simple question: "In what way would it help my paper mill to hire you as an employee?" What will your answer be?

Have you got an answer? Or will you delve into your mathematical knowledge so that you produce an answer that is more related to the academic world than it is to the practical one? In this case your answer should be related to the company. You must be able to demonstrate that your discipline will help them in a specific way. If you have researched the area thoroughly and thought about the matter beforehand, you will have no problem impressing the interview panel.

Science

Many experiments conducted in academic institutions are based on the rationale that experimental elegance is far more important than practical applications. For this reason, science graduates can be lulled into a false sense of security when approaching the job market. Job applicants must be able to explain their technologies to the layperson in ordinary language. It took many years for scientists to make it crystal clear to farmers that there were enormous benefits to be gained from milk pasteurisation and hygiene.

Science has to be a means to an end rather than an end in itself. *You must make the interview panel aware of what you have to offer in tangible terms.* Saying you have an extensive knowledge of computer languages is of little use if an employer does not understand the benefits of the computer. If you are asked how your knowledge can help the company do not give a contorted explanation about the relative advantages of one computer language over another. You will not be taken on by an employer who has no knowledge of this area. You may think that it is sufficient for the technical person on the panel to understand you but this is not so. *Very often it is the non-technical person who is the owner or the manager of the firm.* You need to convince him that what you have to offer is really the equivalent of money in the bank. He will have the final word and he wants people who can explain technologies and approaches in an unambiguous way.

There are many other careers where new entrants can have the false impression that they may use the academic jargon freely for the purpose of bringing about solutions. Such fields include those of psychology, sociology, personnel management, accountancy and finance. You have got to translate what you have learned into a medium that makes it operational. In a sense you may have to unlearn all you have learned in order to make it usable. It would be wrong to say that you ought to forget all you have learned in academic institutions. They are the very fountains of knowledge and have acted as the initiators of many progressive developments in modern times. Your function, however, is to make sense of what you have learned and make it highly marketable for yourself in the interview situation. This is not as difficult as you think and you will be surprised at the results you will achieve if you concentrate on this activity.

Marketing your Skills

'Marketable' Knowledge

The nature of the technical knowledge that you will require depends very much on the position. If the company is fabricating silicon chips you will need to know about the different methods of conducting such activities. An ex-tensive knowledge of the process is not required. You do need a knowledge that will convince the interviewers that you are cabable of applying your theoretical background to the solution of practical problems.

If you are applying to a company that is engaged in making devices for the control of noise emissions you must be able to talk about the various theories of noise control. You may be able to give an example of what you mean by referring to a project which you have undertaken on noise control in modern printers. For example, if you have completed a project in this area and discovered what the best and most economical way of doing this is, you should be able explain this in layman's language.

In the case of the career of pilot, interviewees are often asked about the various parts of the aeroplane.

Any good encyclopedia will give you the knowledge you require. If you want to impress you should look up this information before the interview. Applicants for civil engineering jobs and other such careers in the construction field should carefully study engineering drawings to obtain an outline idea of what they will be expected to do. Mechanical, electrical and electronic engineering applicants should, at some stage, have taken a machine apart and should be able to talk freely about the problems they encountered.

Surveys and Projects

Surveys carried out in a school project or as a marketing graduate are 'excess baggage' in the interview context unless you can explain exactly what you did. *You must clarify how the approach you adopted or the findings you established can help the company.* It is not so difficult for you to translate your projects from academic language into the language of the marketplace.

If you have carried out research using random sampling, control and experimental groups, as well as sophisticated data analysis, you may very well be an expert in the particular field. However, your expertise will remain locked up inside in your head or, worse still, in a university library if you don't try to explain it in simple terms. Remember, when such research projects are explained in a clear and concise way at an interview, they place you at an enormous advantage and they will help you to impress. For this reason, you should not make little of the projects you do at second or third level. You must extract the maximum amount of benefit from them for yourself. It may well be the way you went about the project or the places you searched for information that will impress the panel. It is not for you to judge the relative merits of your own project or extra curricular activities in the interview situation. You may safely leave that to the panel. *They want to know whether the skills you have acquired will enhance their profits.* Entrepreneurs and business people are constantly on the look out for new ways of doing things, so that they can get an edge on their competitors.

The business graduate has got to ask himself/herself: "What did I do of a practical nature during my college years where I used the knowledge I gained on my academic course?" Quite a number of graduates give a negative answer to this type of question and tend to dismiss the whole academic training as "a waste of time". It is a great mistake to give this type of answer, even if you feel it is true. You should be able to demonstrate a number of practical ways in which the facts you learned can be applied to the real world. This means that while you are on such courses you should make constant efforts to apply your knowledge to the world around you. *Similar to the fields of engineering and science, you have got to dejargonise yourself or you won't survive in the interview setting.* The business profiles sketched below will give you an idea of how other graduates in the engineering and business areas have succeeded in impressing interview panels with the courses and skills they had.

Analysis of Activities

Apart from saying that you participate in certain leisure activities it is a most valuable exercise for you, personally, to look into why you became involved in these activities in the first instance, what exact contribution you made to the achievement of the goals of the group, how and by whom the activities were organised, monitored and controlled and what you believe you gained from such activities. If you examine these areas closely you will accumulate a wealth of information not only about yourself but about the world around you and how you, yourself, would function in a job situation. The answers to the question about how you became involved in an activity relate to such matters as those focused on in the following analysis.

Self-analysis of your Involvement in Group Activities

Ask yourself if your involvement is related to:
* the friends you have;
* your desire for independence or involvement;
* your desire to relax;
* the need to help people;
* your wish for fulfilment;
* your altruism;
* your generosity.

With regard to the contribution you made you could talk in a balanced way about:

- the achievement of some notable victory;
- your part in holding the group together;
- how your understanding of the leader's needs and requests assisted the group;
- the special knowledge which you had that contributed to the group's success.

A clear analysis by you of how the leaders of the group carried out their roles could be conducted under headings such as:

- the amount of delegation that was used;
- the personality strengths and weakness of the leaders;
- the qualifications which they brought to their positions;
- an overall evaluation of their contribution to the group's success or otherwise.

You should also look closely into what you gained from the group with respect to:

- actual new knowledge you acquired;
- how things ought to be organised;
- what you learned from the failures of the group;
- what areas you would have focused on in order to make the activity even more successful than it was.

It must be stressed that the activity can be anything from chess playing to organising a rock concert. You can learn something from all human activities in which you participate and interviewers are extremely anxious to know what you learned from these activities. Most people do not reflect on what they are doing at all and it is in this respect that the good interview candidate can score well, if he/she takes the time to reflect and prepare the answers. It doesn't really matter what activity you are talking about.

If you are applying for a position in personnel, for instance, and the only personnel activities that you were ever involved in were classroom-based ones, you have got to be able to talk about matters such as group cohesion or lack of it, problems that arose and how they were resolved, your relationship with the class group, your friends and peers, leadership roles within the group, different attitudes and philosophies that the group had, how the total group related with other groups and so on. You need to be able to show how these activities can be applied to solving problems in work situations. The principal characteristics that the applicant needs for a career in personnel are awareness of and sensitivity to others. Interviewers usually feel that they are fully qualified to gauge these matters on the basis of your responses to questions.

KEY CONCEPTS

- Before people get to know you, get to know yourself.

- You can rectify your weaknesses.

- Make your knowledge 'user-friendly'.

- Clarify for yourself the benefits of group activities.

3

Arm Yourself With Knowledge

It goes without saying that applicants for jobs have got to know the technical side of their jobs, as well as the more human side. The problem for the interviewee is to decide whether such knowledge is useful or not. For this reason, the concepts have to be explained in layman's terms. *Job prospects can be enhanced quite considerably if applicants sell themselves and their skills at interviews through translating what they have learned on academic courses into clear tangible benefits for employers.* It will suffice to mention a few specific areas from the social service fields.

Nurses need to know about the treatment of illness, the drugs that are to be used, the new medical equipment that has been introduced into hospitals, differences between age groups, the appropriateness of different treatments, all the criteria for evaluating levels of sickness, the symptoms of diseases, signs of deterioration and improvement as well as recent research into their particular areas of specialisation.

Teachers have to keep abreast of such matters as approaches to teaching, audio visual aids, research into learning procedures, computerisation, remedial measures, significant educational experiments, discipline, the legal status of schools, insurance, testing theory and evaluation procedures, the nature of intelligence and practical learning approaches.

Policemen and women need to know about the law, psychological research into criminal behaviour, modern measures of detection, physiological studies, computerised communication systems and data analysis, electronic methods of traffic control, robotics, security systems, international terrorism and current affairs.

These should be very familiar terms to applicants for such positions. Naturally, in most cases, such applicants will have heard of these concepts and will be using them in essays, examination questions and even in discussions.

Researching Effectively

In order to clarify the type of research you need to undertake examples are given from five of the main career areas which span most of the job market. They are:
1. caring and medical;
2. engineering;
3. science;
4. general;
5. commerce and secretarial.

It is not intended to cover these fields in depth but, rather, to sketch the essential kind of information that an interview applicant needs to have if applying for a position in any of these fields. *If you intend to apply for careers outside of these categories you need to gather the essential knowledge in a similar way.*

Make the knowledge you have of your own field of interest, and the further specific career information outlined below, as tangible and 'user-friendly' as possible. Included are a number of career profiles that are related to people who were successful in job interviews precisely because of their ability to impress interview panels.

The Caring and Medical Professions

People who work in all of the helping professions are expected to have certain person-orientated characteristics that make them particularly suitable for their positions. The careers include those of nurse, physiotherapist, psychologist, counsellor, teacher, social worker, dentist and doctor.

Interview panels will want to know how good you are with people and how well you relate to them. Since the only way that your personality orientation can be established is through examining your behaviour, a great deal of the interview is going to be taken up with teasing out why you became involved in different kinds of activities and why you made specific kinds of decisions. For this reason, you need to be very clear on your reasons for wanting to become a nurse, a psychologist or a counsellor.

It is not sufficient to state merely that you are interested in people. You need to illustrate this by referring to your extra curricular work with old or young people, your participation in a drama group, how you became involved in a debating society, what team sports you play, the benefits of socialising with others. Your life experiences will be different to everyone else's and if you are applying for one of the caring professions you have got to get this message across. The intending teacher would want to be able to say how she/he has participated in children's picnics, the scouts, an operatic or ballet society, a community project or other such interactive programmes.

The interviewers are, generally, not prejudiced about what the applicant has been involved in, provided that it is centred around people. You will agree that it is most unreasonable of job applicants to expect that they will be given caring roles if they don't have experience of this area. It is not acceptable for a person who is applying for a position as a trainee nurse to have no experience of any type of group activity.

The Career of Doctor

A great deal of the preparation for careers in medicine occurs under the umbrella of scientific research. The reason for this is, of course, the scientific basis that underlies medical treatment. Invariably, the academic entrance requirements for medical schools around the world are very exacting but, when medical graduates are being interviewed for various positions, their personalities, attitudes, ethics and beliefs are often every bit as important as their knowledge of medicine.

In recent years there is a growing awareness of the detrimental effects of prescribed drugs and, for this reason, medical interview panels want to know what non-medical skills and characteristics the intending doctor will bring to the job. Depending upon the hospitals to which you apply, questions will be asked related to their specialisation and your judgement will be assessed on the answers you give.

Other areas that will be teased out include your knowledge of medical ethics and the law as it relates to medicine and moral issues. Furthermore, due to the fact that public health consumes a large amount of public funds you will be expected to have an understanding of how Health Boards operate.

On the following pages you will find career profiles illustrating how interview decisions were made in particular cases. It is interesting to note how experience, outside the qualification, had an influence on the final choice.

Career Profile: Doctor

P G qualified as an MD in 1976. She worked as a Senior House Officer at maternity and women's hospitals and later in the accident and emergency department in surgery in a city hospital. After further experience in both general and emergency surgery she offered her services as a surgeon to the Palestinian refugee camps in the Lebanon and arrived at Bourji Al-Baranjineh in 1985. Except for a brief visit home during 1986, she remained at Bourji Al Baranjineh throughout the desperate siege until the camp was relieved in 1987. Subsequently, she was interviewed for a senior position in a large hospital in the UK. She feels it was the recounting of her experiences and the manner in which she resolved problems, without the necessary medical supports, that convinced the interview panel to appoint her as Senior House Surgeon.

Engineering

There is some confusion in people's minds about what constitutes an engineer. The craftsman, the mechanic, the construction technician and the professional engineer are all classified as engineers.

What should be kept in mind is that the engineering discipline should be looked upon as covering a wide spectrum of activity that goes from the most creative and cerebral side to the most practical and repetitive. The applicant for a job in engineering should be fully aware of where he/she stands in this spectrum.

The professional engineer who has no understanding of the contribution which the technician can make to a project team or the technician who doesn't appreciate the co-ordinating role of the professional engineer will both make poor employees.

The branches of engineering include aeronautical, agricultural, automobile, bio-medical, building services, chemical, civil and structural, computer information, control and measurement, electrical and electronic, environmental, fuel, mechanical, mining and mineral, naval, architectural, marine and production. Even though these divisions seem to be very neat, they don't represent the real situation because one discipline can flow into another very easily so that such divisions become blurred.

You should be very much aware of your own specialisation, while at the same time being conscious of where this specialisation fits into the overall engineering discipline. You must know the notable trends in the engineering field. It is clear, for instance, that 'solid state electronics' is becoming a fundamental factor in modern engineering. All engineers need to have a knowledge of electronics and computerisation if they are to function fully in their own areas.

Profiles of a number of people working in engineering fields will give you a good idea of the kind of information of which you need to be aware when sitting for an interview for such positions. Ask such people what exactly they do and you will acquire clues to the knowledge that you need to convince the interviewers that you are the person for the job. Here are a few examples of engineers whose profiles you need to match if considering positions in this profession. The activities are humdrum enough but if you can identify elements of your training/academic programmes which are similar to these you will then be in a position to sell yourself effectively. Job applicants are frequently asked about faculty projects, work experience and other practical applications of the knowledge they have accumulated. They needed backgrounds in engineering in order to perform well in their chosen career areas. To impress at the interview, they also needed an appreciation of how their academic knowledge fitted in with the work environment.

Career Profile: Communications Engineer

E M works in transmission performance with a telephone company. She looks at the quality of the customer's perception of a transmission. Much of the work involves testing with members of the public. The company's aim is to develop objective scientific transmission measures. It is a complex task, the ear notices some types of background noises more than others and sometimes prefers low noise on a line to silence. The results of her research enabled her to impress her employees that she was suitable for promotion to research and development.

Career Profile: Design Engineer

S K says that the year he spent in the design/drawing office of a Water Authority, as a part of his engineering course, was most beneficial and it was one of the areas he was able to talk about in the interview for his present job as an inspector for a mineral water company.

Both of these graduates had completed degree courses which fitted in with the job specifications for the positions for which they were applying. E M was able to explain to the panel what kinds of trouble shooting problems had arisen in his degree project, whereas S K's experience was concerned with drawing.

Science

In many ways the science area is very similar to engineering and it is common to find highly qualified science graduates working in the same fields as engineers.

Of course, in the science discipline also, it is necessary for technicians and degree holders to know how their knowledge can be applied to the real world. Numerous technologies have developed around the sciences and the more important include computer technology, biotechnology, the pharmaceutical industry, enzyme technology, instrumentation, bio-medicine and medical technology, chemical engineering, environmental engineering and studies, pollution control, food processing and technology, agricultural technology and engineering.

It is very important for science graduates to be able to explain how the scientific method can be used for the solution of problems in the business setting. Job applicants for positions in scientifically or chemically orientated industries need to be able to clarify how the isolation of problem areas, the gathering of scientific data, the testing of theories and the discovery of new solutions can assist the entrepreneurial firm in its day to day work.

The research and development function is particularly the province of the scientist and it is vital for the intending science job applicant to be able to explain how research methods, in which he/she has become proficient at university or technological college, can benefit the firm to which he/she is applying.

If you look at some of the careers in which people with science qualifications are engaged, you will get a good idea of what you need to know.

In the case of all work-related activities, the job applicant has got to look at knowledge from the perspective of employers. They are not interested in finding out the mathematical formulae that lie behind the problem solving theories. They want jobs to be done and goods to be sold at the proper time, as well as in the most economical and competitive way. Therefore, your mind-set has got to be different to the purely academic mind-set. You have to think costs, overheads and practical applications, while you think solutions and offer benefits that are compatible.

> ### Career Profile: Software Engineer
>
> *B M, BSc (Computer Science) works with the business communications division of a telecommunications firm and divides his time between maintaining existing software and enhancing systems on behalf of customers. The communications division maintains a 24-hour fault reporting system for private circuits, such as those in banks. They write high-level design, produce the software and test it, until everyone is satisfied. In his interview B M needed to be able to explain his technical knowledge in practical terms, so that he could show he could communicate with customers.*

General

This classification is being used to include other areas that job applicants can enter either after, or sometimes during, periods of second level education. Many of these fields can also be entered after completing a university or technological course. They include careers in banks, insurance, the police, the civil service, accountancy, the trades, the retail trade, transport, security, journalism and many others. It is a category in which applicant selection is made on the basis of a certain minimum standard of education and good interview performance. The individual interviewer, or the interview panel, cannot assume that the candidate before them has a high level of academic ability, as is the case with the university or the technological college graduate. For this reason, far more emphasis is put on the interview and the job applicant has to sell himself/herself in a once-off situation. The outlines of essential information given in the following pages will help to clarify what minimum amount of knowledge is required about any general job.

Use the Following Checklist to Expand your Knowledge

Below is a checklist of what you need to know about the companies or organisations to which you are applying.

- Size of company or organisation.
- Assets.
- Number of employees.
- The name of the present Managing Director.
- Business activities in which the company is involved.
- Professional work the organisation does.
- How the work is carried out.
- Recent developments in the company or organisation.
- Recent developments in the industry or field of activity.
- Acquisitions that are pending or have been effected.
- Managerial functions that are represented in the company or organisation.
- Principal competitors.
- How current economic, political, social and cultural matters may affect the company.
- The ethos of the company or organisation.
- The legal status of the company or organisation, whether sole trader, limited, public, semi- State or State owned.

Banks:Essential Information

- When you open a current account in a bank you are normally given a cheque book. This type of account does not usually earn you any interest if you are in credit, but you have got to pay interest on it if it is overdrawn.
- The deposit account is the type of account that is used when you wish to leave money in the bank that you don't want to use immediately. This earns interest at the current rate.

- Customers can have what is called a term loan or an overdraft facility. A term loan refers to a specific period of time and has to be paid back within whatever period is specified. An overdraft facility is also for a stated amount but there is usually no fixed term for repayment, unless specified.
- Borrowers are often asked for some security such as the deeds of a house as a form of collateral. This type of loan is known as a mortgage.
- Banks are regulated by the Central Bank which insists on standard procedures being followed.
- The Governor of the Central Bank is appointed by the government and, in this way, the government tries to exert some control over expenditure.
- The banks are commercial institutions which are expected to make a profit. For this reason they will give better facilities to customers who have higher rates of creditworthiness.
- Most banks are anxious to promote business and employment, and, for this purpose, they have business management units staffed by those who understand the needs of business.
- Loans are given out to viable businesses, if they provide an adequate business plan and realistic business projections.
- The banks conduct reviews of business performance from time to time in order to ensure that the money they have invested is safe.
- The principal competitors of the banks are building societies, credit unions, insurance companies and various other lending agencies.
- In future years all European banks will compete on an equal footing.

Insurance: Essential Information

- Insurance is a very comprehensive service provided for people who wish to protect themselves against loss of property, life or earnings.
- It covers the full range of accidents or problems that can occur in a person's life. For this reason, the kind of information that the applicant for a position with an insurance company needs is very extensive but, usually, the interviewers are satisfied if the applicant shows an awareness of the kinds of areas that are mentioned here.

- Even though the client takes out insurance cover to protect himself/herself against accidents, the insurance companies have got to take the view that they are working in a commercial environment. For this reason, every risk has to be gauged on its merits.
- The insúrance company is anxious to minimise its risks and to maximises the amount of profit that it makes. Therefore, companies are anxious to become involved in the most lucrative side of the market and to avoid areas where they are likely to lose money. It is well known, for instance, that motor insurance is a most unprofitable area to be involved in because of the kinds of awards that are being made by the courts.
- Public liability cover is also a high risk area for the same reason. Any situation where there is a danger to life and limb tends to be avoided by the insurance company. The applicant for positions with insurance companies needs to be extremely conscious of such high risk areas.
- In the case of life assurance cover, the job applicant needs to know about the latest research into diet and the effect it has on health. High risk people include those who smoke or drink too much. Obviously, being HIV positive has become a high risk area in recent years and the insurance companies are not anxious to cover people who have this condition.
- Certain occupations have entered the category of 'high risk' status because of the high levels of stress attached to them. There is a higher incidence of early deaths among some occupations. The job applicant for an insurance company needs to know this.
- In the case of public liability cover, certain activities are regarded as riskier than others. These can include swimming, boating, horse riding, roofing and tiling and using electrical equipment. All of these areas need to be studied by the job applicant. This information can usually be found by merely asking for copies of the various policies with which the insurance company deals.

Police Force: What you Need to Find Out

- What the work consists of.
- The kinds of activities in which the police are engaged.

- What they are required to know.
- How the members of the police force interact with other people.
- The personal characteristics the good officer needs to have.
- The court system.
- The way the law operates.
- People's legal and civil rights.
- How to interview people.
- The kinds of activities that young people are interested in, as well as many other related areas, can be learned about quite easily by talking to a police officer.

Commerce and Secretarial

In a certain sense, many jobs can be categorised under the term 'commerce' because it is the profit motive that drives all companies and many organisations.

The term is used here to cover career areas that have a specific commercial or business bias. A useful way of classifying such careers is by considering the way companies are structured through various functions, such as marketing, finance, production, purchasing, sales, personnel and technical. If you are applying for a job under such headings you need to keep the interdependence of such functions in mind.

None of these functions can exist in a vacuum and an applicant for a position in any of them has got to know the total purpose of the company. Therefore, if you are applying for a position in the financial department of a company you have got to be aware of where the financial function fits in. Similar to the other areas described above you must be able to explain how accountancy concepts such as cost analysis, quantitative analysis and financial forecasting will work out in practice for the firm to which you are applying. Indicators of business success and levels of economic activity, such as GDP, GNP, opportunity costs, the liquidity ratio, rates of inflation and deflation, short-term, medium-term and long-term predictions, pump priming, exchequer borrowings and receipts, as well as the various forms of taxation, are also important. Interviews for civil service positions are usually conducted by a special appointments commission which is made up of experts from various walks of life.

Positions for administrative and clerical officers are filled from the ranks of school leavers who have to undergo comprehension, general knowledge and mathematics tests as well as a broadly ranging interview that focuses on:

- current affairs;
- knowledge of government;
- awareness of socio-cultural and political developments in the country and abroad.

For a more detailed description of the civil service interview, see page 74 below.

Secretarial

Secretarial positions don't fit neatly into any category because the work spans the whole spectrum of business activity. For this reason the knowledge that a secretary needs to have will be closely connected with the particular organisation to which he/she is applying. This will have to be researched under guidelines given earlier in this chapter. Thus, if a secretary is applying for a position with a building company, the kind of information needed will be quite different to the information needed if applying to an insurance company.

At the same time, there are certain skills of an interpersonal nature that all secretaries need to have. These skills can often be of a very high order because the secretary in modern companies has to deal with all facets of the organisation's activities. At one level the secretary is the person who types all the letters, answers all the telephone calls, keeps the office in order and at the same time makes the coffee for the staff. At another level, the secretary can be considered to be essential. He/she frequently knows all the sources of information which are required for making highly sophisticated decisions. The secretary is usually the person who fronts the organisation and, because of this, can acquire enormous status and authority.

You must watch for opportunities to make even a casual remark which can show your interviewer that you have taken trouble with the preparation of the interview.

All occupational areas need to be researched, so that the intending interview applicant can demonstrate at the interview that he/she has gone to a good deal of trouble in order to find out about the job for which they are applying. Remember, it is evidence of research, rather than actual facts and figures, that the interview panels are most interested in. You are not expected to be an encyclopedia of knowledge nor are you expected to have an in-depth knowledge of the job in question.

If you make a concerted effort to find out about the position for which you are applying and if you can demonstrate that you have made this effort, you will find that the interviewers will be very satisfied with you. When this line of approach is adopted and if you have taken the trouble to draw up a proper career profile and analysis of your own skills, the self confidence that this results in will give you a head start over others who are not quite clear about what their aims are and who have very little idea about what the position is all about.

If you come armed with solid facts, tangible evidence of your strengths and the ability to sell yourself and your skills to the company you will impress the panel.

Look closely at the academic qualifications you have and draw tangible connections between the subjects you have studied and the job for which you are applying. You will be surprised at the connections you will find when you look for them.

However, impressing the interview panel is one thing, taking control of the interview is quite a different matter that requires the synchronisation of many different skills. The next chapter deals with the question of taking control of the interview in such a way that you will enhance your chances of being selected for the job you want.

KEY CONCEPTS

- There are human as well as technical dimensions to all jobs.

- Effective research is a crucial factor in interview success.

- Understand the relevance of your knowledge to most jobs.

- Thorough research leads to an effective interview performance.

4

Taking Control

The title of this chapter may seem to be a bit ambitious because, where interviews are concerned, all the obvious advantages are on the interviewers' side: the interviewers decide what questions are going to be asked, they compile the agenda that is going to be followed and they are in the position of being able to reward the job applicant who fits in with their idea of what is required.

The job applicant has got to find the right answers. He/she does not appear to have any control over the agenda and comes to the interview board as a supplicant seeking favours, rather than as an advocate demanding rewards. At first glance the encounter seems to be very unequal indeed. Job applicants could be forgiven for believing that nothing at all can be done to control the situation. Nonetheless, it is well known that certain measures, which can be practiced by interview candidates, greatly assist the establishment of rapport between them and employment interviewers. Apart from knowing about yourself and knowing the job well, how you comport yourself physically is one of the main components in establishing a good rapport with people and is one of the most powerful influences in interpersonal relationships. It is often said that, for success in the employment interview, how you look is more important than what you know.

Posture and Movement

If you study the posture and gestures of influential people who control or influence others around the world, you will be struck by the emphasis that is placed on gestures and movement. Charismatic people, such as Pope John Paul II and Pavarotti, use their hands in open gestures when trying to attract the support of large crowds. It is not suggested that you should use your arms or body movements in the same way during the interview, but certain gestures are extremely effective when they are per-formed in tandem with compatible verbal statements. Con-versely, statements that are completely out of line with your gestures will almost certainly cost you a lot of marks in the employment interview.

The Influence of Eye Contact

It isn't a case of staring at the interviewer from start to finish. Indeed, you have to be careful not to function in this way. Neither is there a problem about blinking or about turning your eyes aside momentarily while you try to answer a question. It is regarded as extremely rude and domineering to try to outstare someone else.

When Does the Interview Start?

Your interview starts outside the door of the room where the interview is taking place because you have got to knock before you go in. Your steps towards taking control begin at this stage. Therefore, you have got to think of the non-verbal cues that emanate from you as you enter the room and approach the interview table. Think of the interaction between you and the interview panel as a form of impression management. This has a great deal to do with how you appear physically so you will need to keep the pointers below in mind. For this reason, you need to focus all your attention on presenting yourself in the best possible light.

You have got to think positively and confidently about yourself and how you are going to influence the outcome of the interview as soon as the opportunity presents itself. You should also try to have a real interest in meeting the people who are about to interview you. In this way, you will have the desired impact and establish the essential rapport between yourself and the panel that will lead to a successful outcome.

Pointers for Maximum Initial Impact

- Knock at the door before you enter. Don't try to break down the door and don't scratch it furtively.
- Make sure you draw yourself up to your full height, don't slouch, and keep your hands out of your pockets. If you bring a folder with a copy of your CV and references this will give you something to hold and may be useful to the interviewer.
- Approach the interview table confidently, taking care not to drag your feet, march, strut or lurch forward.

- Shake hands with the interviewer in a firm but unforceful manner.
- Sit on the chair you are offered.
- If you are not asked to sit down request permission after a short pause.
- Sit fully into the chair with your back laid properly against the back rest.
- Place the palms of your hands on your knees and wait for the interview to begin.
- Look attentively at the interviewers whether they are looking at you or not. Inattention and lack of concentration are often sensed rather than observed.

Pointers for Appropriate Posture and Eye Contact

- Don't stretch your hands out like an orator addressing a crowd when listing your hobbies.
- When you are speaking, coupling your palms as you would when holding a football is one way of getting the message across that you are a thoughtful person who can carry out a plan of action.
- Don't stare at the interviewers in such a way that you cause them embarrassment while they search their minds to ask you further questions.
- Blink if you have to. In normal relationships eye contact is maintained for between 30 and 60 seconds only, often for less.
- Always look intently at the interviewer when being asked a question.
- It is acceptable to turn your eyes aside while searching for the proper answer.
- If you want to control the interview you must be certain to look fearlessly at the panel while you deliver a balanced answer and wait for the next question with an eager look of interest on your face.

Taking control means steering the interview in a direction that is as familiar as possible to you. You need to enlist the sympathy and approval of the interviewer. Therefore, you have got to take whatever steps are necessary to make the communication between you smooth and productive for both of you. In a sense you need to get to know the interviewer as well as he/she gets to know you. The interviewer does not appreciate being put under pressure by you and expects to have a relatively pleasant time while talking to you. You have got to keep in mind that this is no ordinary conversation and that your total performance, including answers, non-verbal cues and the questions you may ask, are being constantly evaluated in the interview process.

Importance of Good Non-verbal Cues

Keep in mind that researchers have found that job applicants in an employment interview are rated more highly when they practice the following.

- Greater eye contact.
- Smiling.
- An attentive posture.
- Relevant gestures.
- A shorter distance between interviewer and interviewee.
- Keeping the interviewee's body directly in line with that of the interviewer.

Research has also shown that, using these techniques, you will be perceived and rated as:
- more likely to be accepted;
- more successful;
- more qualified;
- better liked;
- more desirable;
- more motivated;
- more competent;
- more satisfied if given the position.

If these statements are even only half true they indicate clearly how careful you must be about the signals you give to the interviewer.

KEY CONCEPTS

- Remember that the interviewer is human and he/she likes to have a continuous flow of conversation rather than to be constantly jerking from subject to subject.

- The tendency of interviewers to follow a pattern should help you to plan what you are going to say and to anticipate many of the questions you may be asked.

- If you don't know the answer to a question say that you don't know but know where the information can be found.

- Don't talk for too long without getting a response from the interviewer.

- Don't respond to an invitation to tell the interviewer about yourself by a question such as "What do you want to know?"

5

Communication Styles

Just as interview candidates have different personalities, interviewers also have different styles of communication. The fact that such styles of communication can, to a certain extent, determine the general thrust of an employment interview makes it imperative that you should have an understanding of how interviewers differ.

It is important to discover whether the interviewer is motivated by a direct, no nonsense, black and white, rational, fact-accumulating, technical and, possibly, narrow or intolerant mind-set, or an indirect, liberal, broad, probing, open-ended one.

Directive Style

If the interviewer favours the directive style of interviewing the job applicant must be quite clear about facts and not wander very much from the questions that are being asked.

Such interviewers do not like job applicants to give opinions when they are being asked for solid facts. It is expected that the job applicant will have a good deal of knowledge about the job, will avoid what such interviewers regard as 'waffle' and won't allow their replies to be punctuated by mannerisms.

Facts and figures are normally what such interviewers are interested in and this is what you should try to give them. They tend to be extremely impressed if you are knowledgeable about the job, the economy and how your qualifications might apply to the work they have for you.

Normally, interviewers who employ such a style have not been specifically trained in interview techniques and they do not focus on finding out what is behind the answers you give.

There will be a tendency to go from one area to another rather rapidly without much in-depth probing of any area. You, for your part, should not stray from the questions you are being asked.

Such interviews leave many job applicants with a sense of futility at not being able to express themselves in full. However, it is important for you to keep in mind that the interviewer who adopts a directive approach with you will also, very likely, adopt the same approach with every interviewee. In this way, your answers will be given just as much weight as anybody else's and everything will depend on your accuracy and factual knowledge about the job, the company, your skills, the marketplace and other economic criteria.

In general it can be said that managers of companies who have a traditional approach to management and who carry out very little delegation have a certain identifiable approach to interview selection. The hallmarks of this approach tend to be a respect for discipline, education, excellent dress and positive answers. For them it is also vital that applicants are intelligent, have a good knowledge of the job and the ability to withstand pressure.

Interviewers of this kind are not impressed by what may be regarded as interview skills and they don't like job applicants to gesticulate a lot while they are talking. At the same time, they would prefer that candidates aren't immobile in front of them. Such interviewers are frequently interested in job applicants' family backgrounds, where their brothers and sisters are working and appearance. The applicant's ability to take instructions, to sell themselves well and the condition of their health are also important to these directive interviewers.

Guidelines for Success in Dealing with the Directive Style

- Stick to your guns.
- Don't stray from the topic.
- Give facts and avoid comment.
- Watch your eye contact.
- Be brief.
- Don't mumble.
- Know the company and the specific job well.
- Cover all inconsistencies in your CV related to subjects in which you underscored or which you dropped.

Examples of Closed Questions

- Where did you go to school?
- What age are you?

- What salary do you expect?
- How many years' experience have you at this kind of work?
- Which optional subjects did you do for your final examinations?

Suggested Answers for the Above Closed Questions

- I am ... years of age.
- I attended ... second level school.
- I expect a salary of ... .
- Three years.
- Business organisation, accountancy and French.

Tips for Coping with Closed Questions

- These are direct questions that require very precise answers and no interviewer will thank you if you give detailed replies.
- In general , these questions come at the start of an interview.
- Closed questions may be asked, unexpectedly, in the middle or at the end of the interview and you must respond briefly to them.
- There is usually only one correct answer to a closed question.

Confrontationalist Style

Closely allied to the directive style is the confrontationalist style. Indeed, many job applicants would consider the directive approach to interviewing to be highly confrontationalist. This is a mistake, because interviewers can be quite directive and still not be confrontationalist. What is meant by the confrontationalist approach to the employment interview is a deliberate policy by the interviewers, or the interview panel, to try systematically to provoke the candidates into responding negatively to questions they are being asked.

The questioning is confrontationalist and deliberately introduced into an interview in order to gauge your reactions. The interviewers do not really expect you to agree with them. You are expected to respond and it is critically important that you do so. The questions ahead will give you an idea of what to expect.

Examples of Confrontationalist-style Questions

- "You don't think that you are the right person for the job, do you?"

- "We don't think you have the right qualities for the position."

- "Do you not think that your examination results are very weak?"

- "Can you give one good reason why we should employ you instead of any one of the other 200 people who applied for the job?"

To the First Question above you might say:

- "Well, in fact, I think I am one of the most suitable candidates you can find because my qualifications are the ones that you asked for and I am capable of fitting in with a team as my involvement with the school football (hockey, etc.) team shows."

or

- "I know that I will be an asset to your company because I have some ideas about how performance might be improved."

The other questions should be handled in a similarly positive manner. If you adopt such a frame of mind when dealing with these questions you will gain the maximum benefit from them. In any case, the interviewers expect you to respond positively and to cope with the negative implications in their questions. You must have done your homework in order to be able to give these answers because you may very well be asked to elaborate on what you are saying. If you can't elaborate and you are being interviewed by a directive and confrontationalist interviewer your answers will be rated very negatively. It is very difficult for you to know, in advance, which type of interviewer you are going to have. If you concentrate on the questions you are being asked at the beginning of the interview, you may be able to see the direction in which the interviewer wants you to go.

Hallmarks of the Confrontationalist Style

- Questions are normally closed ones and deliberately provocative, e.g. "You don't think you are the right person for this job, do you?"

- Your *reaction* rather than your *knowledge* is being tested.
- The interviewer tends to be very aggressive in an effort to test ability to survive under stress.
- Questions can be open, closed or mixed.
- Such interviews are normally conducted for jobs in security, the army or the airforce where very quick reactions in stressful conditions are required but are also used more generally.

Guidelines for Success

- Stay cool no matter what the provocation.
- Always address yourself to the content rather than the form of the question.
- Always reject implied criticism of yourself in a firm controlled fashion.
- Do not let yourself be brow beaten but don't over respond.
- Keep in mind that you are dealing with a style of interview rather than a rotten interviewer.
- Confrontationalist interviewers know very well that the style they are adopting is purposely aggressive and they will respect you for responding firmly.

Non-directive Style

The opposite of the directive approach is the non-directive one. In theory, the idea behind this style is to allow you to express yourself freely and for the interviewer to be as unobtrusive as possible.

You have got to be extremely careful when such a style is being adopted because you can very easily be led into a false sense of security. Some people regard such interviewers as having a far more fixed agenda in their minds that the directive ones. Furthermore, the interviewer who is using this style may be every bit as directive as the interviewer who asks very direct questions. Many job applicants find this style off putting and they don't really know where they stand after the interview.

The interviewer sets out to put the candidate completely at ease by inviting him/her to smoke, have a cup of coffee, sit back and relax or by talking about the weather, holidays and various television programmes. You must not be misled by this style.

Remember, you are not participating in an ordinary conversation no matter what the interviewer says to you about having a little chat with you. The bottom line is that the interviewer is asking questions, making observations and coming to conclusions about you all the time.

Therefore, even though you should try to fit in with the style that is being adopted, you must focus your answers on the questions that are being asked rather than begin to tell stories about yourself. It is extremely easy to wander away from the point in the non-directive interview.

It would be helpful for you to be able to realise when this style is being consciously used by the interviewer. You can then ensure that your answers are related to the nature of the information being sought. A number of specific techniques are used in the non-directive style and awareness of these will enable you to recognise when it is being used so you can respond accordingly. The techniques include:

• silence;
• probing;
• verbal encouragers;
• restatement;
• clarification.

Silence

In the case of silence the interviewer intends to be helpful by not interrupting you in what you are saying. The usual length of a normal silence is about five seconds. Frequently, when silence goes beyond this time candidates begin to get nervous. If your interviewer leaves large gaps between questions it may be a case that you are being tested for your ability to survive under stress. However, normally you are being given the chance to express yourself.

You must be careful not to ramble when you are afforded this opportunity and if you think you have talked for a sufficiently long time on any subject you should stop. If the silence between you and the interviewer goes over ten seconds, you should probably ask if you are to continue.

Probing

Probing questions are used in order to get you to elaborate on what you have already said.

Verbal Encouragers

These are merely the sounds such as "mmm", "go on" or "I see" which the interviewer emits to encourage you. You can often gauge the approach that the interviewer has from such encouragers.

Restatement

This involves the interviewer restating the interviewee's answers in such a way, and with such a tone of voice, that there is an implied suggestion that the interviewee is to continue. Many find it difficult to cope with this technique because, at times, it can be rather infuriating. If the interviewer makes statements such as "so you worked in the bank during the summer" or "so you found certain aspects of the job rather stimulating" it is really intended that you continue and explain in more detail what you mean.

Clarification

Interviewers will sometimes ask for clarification. This request can be transmitted non-verbally by a quizzical look. You have got to be sensitive to the interviewer's responses and comply with verbal or non-verbal requests for clarification by expanding on your last remark or statement.

This type of interviewer has very likely been trained in counselling techniques and would like you to respond in the appropriate way by explaining yourself. In particular, you have got to keep in mind that if the interviewer is completely committed to this approach you will give the utmost satisfaction if he/she receives reassurance from you that the approach leads to productive exchanges between you. If you respond flatly to the interviewer's efforts at restatement of your comments, you are transferring negative feelings and are unlikely to be rated in a positive way.

Examples of Open Questions

- Tell me about your life at secondary school.
- How do you see your career developing over the next ten years?
- How hard have you worked at your present job?
- How would you describe your leisure-time activities?
- What was your boss like?
- How have you managed to balance your curricular and extra-curricular activities?

Suggested Answers for the Above Open Questions

- My second level school was excellent because of the commitment of the teachers, the range of extra curricular activities, the discipline, the examination results and the prestige of the school.

- In relation to career development, I am a highly motivated person who would like to obtain promotion after an appropriate period of time.

- My present job involved a certain range of problems that I was able to solve, examples of which are. . .

- My leisure time activities taught me characteristics, such as leadership, organisational expertise and social skills, because they were concerned with. . .

- My present boss is a highly motivated and committed person (comments should always be positive rather than negative).

- Extra-curricular activities helped me to broaden my views and gave me an insight into how other people react in different situations.

Tips for Dealing with Open Questions

- The answers which you give to such questions can make or break you, because you haven't the security of dealing with black and white issues as you have in the closed questions. You should not express negative opinions that will land you in the height of trouble. If you hated your boss's guts you need not say so. If you felt you were incarcerated in your second level school, it would be better not to elaborate on the matter, in case the interviewers think that the negative vibes will, eventually, be directed at them.

- What is expected with these types of questions is that you will calmly talk through what your attitudes, feelings and ideas are concerning a range of topics.
- Never answer an open question (such as "Could you tell us a little about yourself?") by asking another question (such as "What do you want to know?"). The interviewer just wants you to talk freely and this what you have to learn to do.

Another way in which questions are divided is into primary and secondary ones. It is useful for the interview candidate to keep this division in mind when responding to the questions.

Primary Questions

These are the questions you are asked that are based on the component stages of the interview. They can include (but are not limited to) the questions concerning the following areas:

- education;
- qualifications;
- work experience;
- expectations;
- knowledge of the job;
- hobbies and interests.

These types of questions are often closed ones initially and they are expanded into open ones as the interview develops. They are frequently based on the CV or application form which you completed and it is imperative that you always keep a copy of any application forms which you have submitted because you will be asked many questions that are based on them.

Secondary Questions

These are questions which seek elucidation of points that have been uncovered through the primary questions. You should conduct a full-scale review of all the likely questions you could be asked on the basis of your answers to the primary questions. Interviewers often use your answers for the purpose of probing subjects to the full in order to get an insight into your coping skills.

Examples of Secondary Questions

- Could you elaborate on what you said about your optional subjects not being suitable for the job at which you were aiming?
- What do you mean where you say in your CV that you learned "how a business operates"?
- What do you think you learned from being captain?
- What is the value of team games?

Secondary questions are often open and candidates should respond to them with plenty of information and elaboration.

Hallmarks of Non-directive Styles

- Questions tend to be open ended.
- Silence is used to test ability to cope under stress or to test initiative.
- Probing questions are used for the purpose of getting interview candidates to elaborate on what they have said.
- Verbal encouragers, such as "mmm" or "go on" are used to gauge ability to develop a theme.
- Restatement is merely a way of getting a candidate to elaborate.
- Clarification may be sought either verbally or with a quizzical look.
- Great emphasis is placed on the candidates' interpersonal skills.

Guidelines for Success

- Since most of the questions will be open rather than closed, make sure you elaborate on your answers.
- Avoid rambling on about things.
- If a period of silence between you and the interview panel becomes too long, ask if you are to continue talking about the last topic under discussion.
- Watch your non-verbal cues.
- Remember non-directive interviewers usually have a specific

agenda that they are following. They will tend to judge more on how you answer rather than on what you say.

Mixed Styles

A further style that can be adopted by interviewers or interview panels is a mixed one consisting of a combination of non-directive and directive techniques. You may find that you are asked to relax, to talk about your leisure interests and the places where you like to go on holidays. Then, you may suddenly be thrown a directive or confrontationalist type of question which catches you completely off guard. Normally, this type of interview doesn't arise when you are being interviewed by one person. However, when there is more than one interviewer involved you may find yourself having to switch from one style to another as the occasion demands. When such a course of action is adopted it is usually in order to establish some specific impression concerning your reactions. These include:

- your ability to adapt to new situations;
- your calmness in difficult circumstances;
- how well you are able to control your emotions.

Jobs in the security industry, the army and the police frequently demand keen responses in such areas. In the next chapter you will read how companies and organisations, such as the police force, vary in their approach to the interview.

KEY CONCEPTS

- Do not give long answers to questions, even if there is an awkward period of silence after you stop talking.

- Do not elaborate too much, even with non-directive styles.

- Make sure you have conducted research on the organisation (see Chapter 3).

- Never try to bluff your way when answering a question given by an interviewer using a directive style.

- Always say you don't know if you can't answer a question from a directive style interviewer.

- Stay calm and use clear, positive and logical reasoning when being questioned by a confrontationalist interviewer.

6

Company Selection Policy

The Relevance of Interview Selection Policy

Frequently, companies will have a certain policy towards selection that can determine, to a large extent, what kind of interview will be conducted and the kinds of personnel selected.

Some companies have, in the past, had a policy of choosing graduates, school leavers, certain age groups, social classes, nationalities, religions, sexes and so on. Many practices of this sort are discriminatory, but many more can depend on the kind of organisation on whose behalf the interview is being conducted.

A good example of organisations that will, very likely, have a specific attitude towards candidate selection are the Christian churches. Since these organisations feel their specific role is to promote a particular set of values, they make no apology for insisting that, for example, intending teachers conform to their philosophy. Job applicants can be asked to sign contracts that oblige them to maintain Christian values and subscribe to the organisation's ethos.

Closely associated with Christian values will be a conformist rather than a reformist attitude to life. Such organisations will want to be sure that you are going to maintain the received wisdom and that you are not going to question its age-worn, established principles and practices. You can, therefore, expect to be questioned about your attitudes to family break up, divorce, separation, contraception, freedom, censorship and many other topics. Should you wish to be employed by such organisations, you need to know what its primary attitudes are and what it considers to be its role in society.

Apart from the churches, other organisations, such as the army, banks, navy, civil service, police, the legal profession and insurance companies, tend to have a strong sense of identity that finds expression in the selection policy adopted. If you wish to establish the philosophy of the company you need to identify the mission statement, i.e. what the central aim of the organisations is. This may be expressed in the annual report or in brochures published by the company.

These organisations invariably have a top down management style where there is little delegation of authority. Many of their management approaches owe far more to tradition than they do to modern insights and practices. You can expect that the line of questioning will be such that your attitudes to tradition, the establishment, structures and superiors will be ascertained at the interview.

It is only to be expected that banks with a 200-year old tradition and insurance companies that helped to fund the Napoleonic Wars would feel they have a special type of ethos. Intending applicants for positions with them should be aware of these influences.

How to Identify an Organisation's Selection Policy

Obviously, if you can have some idea concerning what the company's selection policy is, you will be able to fit in with the job requirements being sought. The guidelines and information sources given below should help you to establish what this policy is.

Career Brochures

These brochures usually clarify the salary scale and the kind of work involved. They will often give you a good 'feel' for the company. Read them and ask yourself the following questions.

- Is the company more interested in its own image than it is in promoting its own products?
- Is there a focus on what the company will do for you or what you can do for the company?
- Does the company identify its own weaknesses as well as its strengths?
- Does the brochure tell you about the pitfalls as well as the benefits?
- How detailed is the careers brochure?
- Does the brochure stress the social side of the company's activities as well as the vocational ones?

Answers to questions, such as those given above, will give you a good idea of how pleasant or otherwise it may be to work with such a company. You will be able to learn whether or not the company has a policy of selecting technical people with a high level of expertise, irrespective of their interpersonal skills. This distinction is important because it will enable you to know where the emphasis should be placed. The following description from a company brochure demonstrates how important some companies feel the social dimension is.

> *The success of CHL Ltd is largely due to the talent and dedication of its employees. This talent not only finds expression in the workplace, but in sports such as soccer, swimming and sailing which have always been popular. The more adventurous become involved in canoeing, water skiing, rock climbing and even parachuting.*

What is important for you is not the kind of activities that are available but, rather, the fact that the company is interested in the total personality. You will find that the selection policy of the company will be very much influenced by such ideas.

The Views of the Founder

Due to the fact that many businesses were the brainchild of a single founder you can often identify the company's selection policy from his/her views. Thus, if a chain of superstores was built by an entrepreneur who left school at sixteen and had to fight hard for a market niche, you can be certain that there will be a strong emphasis on track record and hard work.

The views of founders are often freely available in newspaper commentaries on the business pages. For such organisations the key ingredients of applicants' personalities will be motivation and an interest in innovation. Since the founder had to struggle himself/herself, it is expected that the new employees will be full of ambition to reach the top of the organisational structure.

A leading technological company's promotional brochure has the following mission statement:

We are committed to further growth, to the extent allowed by the recruitment of top quality technical staff who will maintain our reputation for innovation, analytical excellence and sound practical skills.

Such comments reflect the kinds of skills required by an original founder to set up a modern, technological company and he, obviously, would wish others to have the same interest in innovation and entrepreneurship.

Management Structure

The management structure will also give you a good idea about the selection policy that is likely to be adopted. Generally speaking, it can be said that there are two types of structures in organisations. One is the top-down type of structure, mentioned earlier, the other is the flat management structure. In the first type of structure the advised approach is that you should stick carefully to what you are doing. Always obtain approval for your decisions and never stick your neck out. In the second type of structure, management is very interested in delegation and in how much employees are prepared to do for themselves.

If you can establish, in advance, which type of structure the company has, you will be able to know what the selection policy of the company is likely to be. If you find answers to the questions given below you will be well on your way to establishing the selection policy of the company.

- How many separate management functions does the organisation have?
- Are the managers operating their own departments in co-operation with other designated assistants or are they reporting to the MD themselves?
- Do the managers have their own secretaries and does it appear that they have a good deal of autonomy?
- Is the company's organisational chart a detailed and complex one with many functionaries or is it basic?

Job Advertisements

Many job advertisements for vacancies merely state the qualifications and experience required, but some give clues regarding the kind of atmosphere that obtains in the company. The examples given below are taken from a newspaper and it is possible to establish what the selection policy of each company is by examining them carefully.

> *Electronic technician required by large multinational. If you are receptive to training and prepared to adopt a hands-on approach, you could be the person we are looking for.*

This advertisement conjures up an image of a very modern, open and flexible company that is anxious to recruit people who can think for themselves.

> *We are looking for highly qualified chartered accountants. We are a blue-chip company with a solid client base.*

With this type of company, there will be a fairly strong tradition and a philosophy of work that urges conformity to previous standards, target setting and achievements rather than an emphasis on innovation and change.

Words such as 'leading' and 'successful multinational' have certain connotations worth thinking about. They give a very clear insight into what the company thinks about itself and you may be able to 'think yourself' into the sort of philosophy that permeates within the company.

In the case of multinational companies the management structure is likely to be flat, open and based on delegation of responsibilities. At the same time, such organisations can place extreme demands on personnel through their time schedules, production cycles and deadlines. Very often such companies can have an enhanced image of their own ability to innovate. 'Change' may mean change as understood by the company itself only. You must be sure that you understand the management structure of the company and how it has managed change in the past, before you start offering your own recommendations about how the company should operate in the future.

Assess the amount and nature of the information you are given in the advertisement. In some cases job descriptions are quite extensive. This would seem to indicate that the company is very open in its approach but, at the same time, is looking for specific characteristics in the personnel being employed.

For positions in the computer industry, you will be told exactly the languages you are expected to know. When accountants and financial people are being recruited, the advertisements usually refer to the type of work the new recruit will be expected to do. Such work can include auditing, accounts preparation and tax computations. You may be informed that you are required to deal with the following:

- manpower policy;
- organisation planning;
- employee relations;
- remuneration;
- communications.

For technical jobs the advertisements may state that practical experience is needed in fields, such as modern instrumentation technique, production management or maintenance. Apart from specific qualifications and experience, advertisements can often mention personal characteristics, such as:

- initiative;
- drive;
- outgoing personality;
- creativity;
- charisma;
- enthusiasm.

All of these factors are definite clues about the kind of interview you are likely to face. You can often learn what the company wants you to know by reading the job advertisements carefully. Furthermore, you may be able to establish what the precise headings for the interview are likely to be. Usually, if the advertisement outlines the characteristics that successful applicants are expected to have, the interview will be built around such factors. The questions will then be phrased in a manner that is calculated to elicit this information from you. It is vitally important for you to know as much as possible about the company or organisation to which you are applying. Such knowledge will enable you to colour your answers in the appropriate way. If you link the information with an analysis of the performance and structure of the company itself you will have a distinct advantage when attending the interview.

Discrimination and Company Selection Policy

Due to employment equality agencies in many countries and court rulings against discrimination, there are a number of areas about which you are unlikely to be asked. Certain questions are regarded as discriminatory and have resulted in successful litigation by interview candidates. These include questions on whether a woman's husband works, whether the family would suffer if she were not at home to cook the dinner and how she would cope with young aggressive men in the workplace. Other areas where enquiries may not be made relate to:

- arrest, citizenship, spouse's employment, childcare, arrangements or dependents, over generalised enquiries (e.g. do you have handicaps) that do not relate to fitness to perform the job;
- whether the applicant is married, single or divorced, engaged, widowed or any other enquiry on marital status;
- condition of military discharge;
- pregnancy;
- whether the applicant rents the house in which he/she is living.

Questions such as these are not acceptable in democratic countries and are now being ruled out of order. The introduction of a legal ban on such questions in many countries has dramatically changed the whole orientation of many interviews in modern times.

Interviewers and interview panels do not want to be accused of discrimination and, for this reason, tend to ask far more practical and impersonal questions than they did in the past. They will not delve too deeply into your private life because of the employment equality and anti-discrimination laws. The interview focus will, therefore, tend to be on quantifiable and measurable factors that can be substantiated in some way. You can expect that the interviewer is going to follow a set format, not wanting to be accused of asking illegal questions where the possibility of a lawsuit could arise.

Impact of Company Policy on Interview Selection

Apart from styles of communication that interviewers may adopt, quite a number of companies have a specific policy on interviewing which is worth keeping in mind. Interviewers are told to run the interview in a certain way. They are told the problem areas to watch for and they are given guidelines which they are told to follow. Furthermore, a company may have a conscious policy of having their selection undertaken by specialised personnel agencies who run assessment centres.

A study of some company guidelines and how the assessment centres work is most revealing. The following pages describe the kinds of guidelines that are given for the following areas of employment.

1. Insurance and bank interviews.
2. Jobs in education and the police force.
3. Technological or engineering positions.
4. Civil service and general career areas.

These four examples are taken for illustration only so that you will be conscious of the fact that large companies usually have a specific policy towards employment interviews. You should try to establish what this policy is in advance. A study of the four areas outlined below will give all potential job candidates an idea of what interviewers are told to ask you about. The way in which assessment centres work will be dealt with separately in the next chapter.

Insurance and Bank Interviews

Due to the fact that these two types of interviews deal particularly with people and finance, the guidelines that are issued tend to be rather specific in relation to factual data and comprehensive regarding interpersonal relationships.

Professional interviewers in both fields are instructed to question candidates concerning their past work experiences, their ability to handle finance, involvement with insurance and banking and their future goals. Within such areas questions are designed to tap specific activities, e.g. "What exactly did you do in this job or in this activity?" or "In what areas do you think the company you worked for needs to improve?" In addition, questions addressing more intangible areas, such as personal relations are usually included, e.g. "What was your relationship with your co-workers or your fellow students?" or "Can you describe the general way you would like to be living five years from now?" Due to the fact that both of these professions subscribe to employment equality legislation, you may be certain that there will be no sex-related questions, such as those on marital status, child minding and number of dependents.

The most important questions which are asked of the candidates are those which establish the kind of relations they had with fellow classmates and workers. You can expect questions to cover the following areas.

- The level of direct contact you had with customers or buyers.
- Experience with part-time work.
- Attitude towards the bank and insurance companies.
- Whether you can live within your current income.
- How well you can live within your means.
- Your ability to pay your bills on a regular basis.
- In relation to insurance companies especially, the interviewers need to know if you can live on commission.

All financial institutions are interested in matters such as:
- the level of confidence you have that your goals will be reached;
- your ability to persuade people;
- your ability to work without supervision;
- your interest in participating in outside activities and keeping physically and mentally alert;
- many such companies want to know if you have a plan for the future and in what way you see them fitting in with this plan if they employ you;
- insurance companies and banks are particularly interested in your ability to sell yourself on the assumption that if you can do this well, you will be an asset rather than a liability.

Questions similar to those which follow appear in interview guides used by such interviewers and these are followed by the types of reactions and comments which interviewers make afterwards. It is worth seeing yourself from their point of view.

- "How did you happen to get into the organisation you were

working part-time for?"

- "Did you consider other organisations at the time?"

- "Briefly, what did you do in the job or when you were carrying out this function?"

- "Did you have any contact with the public in this job or role? How did this come about?"

- "How did you locate your customers?"

- "What kind of people were you dealing with?"

- "What was your sales record?"

- "How did you compare with others?"

- "How was your schedule of work determined?"

- "What hours did you work?"

- "Did you ever work extra hours? Under what circumstances? How often?"

- "How did you feel about it?"

It is quite evident from these questions that the interviewers want to establish what your level of motivation is as well as your ability to sell and project yourself. Among the comments that bank and insurance interviewers make about people they interview are the following, negative comments.

- "He wasn't selling himself at all."

- "I would want to know what the candidate could do for the company rather than what the company could do for the candidate."

- "She sat back giving a casual, lazy impression which would go against her."

- "She didn't seem like a person who would communicate well with customers."

- "Every answer had to be dragged out of him."

Contrast the above comments with the following, positive interviewer comments.

- "He sticks to his ground."

- "She was able to elaborate."

- "She had done her homework."

- "She knew a lot about the bank."

- "He had good manners."

Jobs in Education and the Police Force

Since jobs in both of these areas are concerned totally with people-oriented problems, these interviewers look for those with interpersonal skills and understanding.

Among the questions school principals are recommended to ask are those dealing with:
- new developments in the educational field;
- the potential teacher's philosophy of life;
- attitudes to authority;
- the ability to adjust;
- interest in young people;
- breadth of interests;
- availability for extra-curricular activity;
- the candidates understanding of his/her own strengths and weaknesses;
- the ability to communicate and overall personality.

As well as these characteristics, police interviewers are also very interested in the potential police officer's ability to deal with stress, to accept rejection, to control his/her own emotions and to cope with failure.

Police interviewers would also like to know how candidates propose to deal with new situations and how adaptable they are. It is particularly important for the potential police officer to have some knowledge of human psychology and how it can be used to advantage.

Questions on levels of motivation are often asked by police interviewers, as well as on the candidate's self discipline and ability to take orders. Since persistence may be an important characteristic in police work, interview panels will want to know what your attitudes and responses are to such questions.

If you have opted out of any areas, such as school subjects, professional courses or games, the interviewers will want to know why. You need to have credible reasons for your actions. The comments below demonstrate that interviewers from different backgrounds bring certain attitudes and approaches with them to the interview situation.

Negative Interviewer Comments

- "He could make people feel ill at ease."

- "She tended to give glib answers."

- "Parents would not feel at ease with her."

- "He would want to boss everyone around."

- "He should smarten up his appearance."

Positive Interviewer Comments

- "She would be a good team person."

- "She would deal with a boss well and would show respect."

- "He seemed to have a moral approach to life."

- "He seems to be a person who wants to educate himself through reading."

- "He was never stuck for an answer which is important in the teaching profession."

In the case of uniformed people, such as army and police personnel, there is a very strong expectation that candidates will adapt themselves fully to the approaches that such organisations have to dress, appearance, formality and public image.

In the educational field, due to the responsibilities involved, the interviewers tend to have very definite approaches concerning the philosophy of life of the candidate and, for this reason, you should be very clear about where you stand on matters such as discipline, sexual relationships, modern trends and religious beliefs. It isn't quite a question of being traditional in your approach but, rather, having the ability to comprehend the significance of changes in young people and to be able to respond effectively to them.

Technological Organisations

Interviewers who interview for technological positions are not interested in technical matters only. They are aware that working with technology can be stressful and, therefore, they will want to find out how adaptable you are. For this reason interviews for such positions will tend to focus a good deal on personality factors, in order to discover how well you will fit in with their structures.

Personality Characteristics

The sample analysis of the selection policy of a technological organisation outlined below is given so that you can be fully aware of the lengths to which these companies go in order to establish whether or not potential employees will be able to cope with the demands that technology can place on their personal resources. The interviewers in this organisation ask questions specifically to establish what the candidate *will do, can do* and *appears to do*.

The first (*will do*) concerns attitudes, motivation, stability, maturity, aptitude and temperament. The second (*can do*) concerns skills, experience, training and education.The third (*appears to do*) concerns dress, poise, appearance, ability to communicate and friendliness.

It is suggested that the best way to measure these qualities is through a planned interview in which questions are asked about work experience, educational background, hobbies, social life, early family experience and goals. Feelings, beliefs and reactions to supervisors, companies, responsibility, work and co-workers should be teased out in order to establish what the candidate's attitudes are.

The degree of effort demonstrated in previous jobs, whether the candidate took the hardest jobs or not, the intensity of the work and the kinds of experiences found to have been valuable are all potential clues to the level of motivation.

The interviewer needs to establish the candidate's stability through finding out how long he/she stayed in the last job, the reasons for job changes, consistency of interests and the ability to follow through, despite difficulties.

Maturity is demonstrated if the candidate takes responsibility for failures, has capacity to get on with others, has emotional control, common sense and foresight. The interviewee needs to realistically accept his/her limitations.

Apart from the knowledge that can be gleaned about aptitudes from formal aptitude tests, some companies feel that aptitudes can be established by asking questions that relate to progress on previous jobs, successes/failures and special talents.

Finally, with regard to temperament, the interviewer should establish what jobs were liked, the reactions to former supervisors, reaction to pressures and the need for people contact.

The same approach to inner characteristics is adopted by the interviewer in relation to the educational field. The inner characteristics that are alluded to above form the basis for this examination as well. Matters, such as the degree of effort demonstrated at school, the ability to complete courses, the acceptance of responsibility, special achievements and the nature of involvement in group activities, are all to be teased out by the interviewer. When considering matters related to the family, these interviewers are asked to explore matters, such as the parents' occupation, what brothers and sisters are doing, main events in formative years, description of upbringing, difficulties needed to be overcome and responsibilities given. Significantly, interviewers are urged to form an overall pattern of the job applicant and to assess his/her ability to do the job. These are some examples of questions.

Attitude

- "How did you feel about your last job?"

- "What was your boss like?"

- "How did you feel about the time you spent at school?"

Motivation

- "How have you managed to balance your curricular and extra-curricular activities?"

- "How hard have you worked in your present job?"

- "How hard did you work at school?"

Stability

- "What was the most difficult course of study you ever undertook?"

- "What led to your decision to leave?"

- "How long have you been interested in this job?"

Maturity

- "Tell me about a work situation in which you lost your cool? What happened?"

- "Have you ever held a formal position in a group?"

Aptitude

- "What special talents do you feel you have?"

- "To what extent do your marks reflect your ability?"

- "Have you any special talents?"

Temperament

- "How would you describe your leadership style?"

- "What do you consider to be the ideal job for you?"

- "How would you describe your approach to leisure activities?"

The Portfolio of Tasks

Since technological organisations employ people to work in areas, rather than at specific tasks, the job description often refers to a range of tasks that are appropriate to what is called a 'portfolio'. Even though the idea of a portfolio of tasks refers to a general concept, it is possible to isolate the factors that will characterise a family of jobs. These characteristics include the following.

- *Organisational structure*, where the job fits into the organisation.
- *Job purpose*, what are the main objectives to be achieved.
- *Responsibilities*, what will the job holder actually do.
- *Conditions*, travel, hours, etc.

- *Critical factors*, what aspects of the job have proved most crucial for success or failure.

The interview should establish how aware the candidate is of these factors. The personal characteristics for the job need to be highlighted so that the interviewer can establish whether candidates have these or not. The characteristics in question will include matters such as education, work experience, abilities, motivation and temperament.

The factor that makes the deepest impression regarding the above instructions to interviewers is the level of unobtrusiveness that is encouraged and the lack of emphasis on technological knowledge. Job applicants can normally expect that such interviews will not deal with technical details to any great extent. It is taken for granted that such people have the required qualifications to carry out the technical side of the jobs in question. However, job applicants ought to be prepared for a number of technical questions in their own fields of expertise as well. Generally, technical questions build upon, or are extensions of, the knowledge which the applicants have already. Applicants are frequently asked how they would apply academic knowledge that they have acquired to the solution of practical problems.

Positions in the Civil and Public Service

Interview panels for careers in the public and the civil service tend to represent a very wide range of interests. If you are being interviewed for a position as an executive officer you will find that you could be facing as many as three interviewers on the one panel. Typically, civil service interviewers ask questions that seem to be very simple and at a superficial level but are, in fact, quite difficult to answer. In the written examinations there is a tendency to ask questions which could be answered by children in primary schools but which give adults many problems.

What the Interviewers Want to Know

You may be asked questions as diverse as the following.

- "What is the population of the country?"
- "What is the name of the present shadow Minister for Finance?"

- "What is the name of the current EC President?"
- "What is the date of the Treaty of Rome?"
- "What is the meaning of EMS?"
- "What is the nationality of Picasso?"
- "What is the current rate of inflation?"

You could have considerable difficulty in answering all of them on the spur of the moment. None of these questions is a difficult one and it is very likely that a 12-year old would be able to answer more of them than you. Therefore, if you are sitting for civil service or public service interviews or examinations, you should keep in mind that you are dealing with interviewers whose job it is to keep up with the times.

It will be vital for you to read the daily newspapers right up to the morning of the interview. These interviewers commonly compile their questions on the basis of the daily news.

Don't be surprised if you are asked about the works of a composer whose music is being performed in the local theatre if you have put music down in your application form as one of your interests.

You should read the sports page carefully if you have stressed sports activities as one of your principal interests, the arts page if you have emphasised these and the literary page if you say that you read a great deal. Such interviewers have little patience with people who profess a great interest in fields of activity which they don't trouble to read about in the daily newspapers.

Questions Asked in Civil and Public Service Interviews

You could be asked a broad range of questions that will test your knowledge of current affairs as they impact on the operation of the country's administrative system. Many of these questions will refer to the current talking points in the civil and public service. Should you really want to prepare well for these interviews, study the relevant journals of the departments in which you are interested in order to establish what the principal concerns are. The following questions refer to some of these issues.

- "What is the role of the public service?"
- "Do you think that you would have much initiative in the public service?"

- "What is the relationship between the political and administrative systems?"
- "What influence does the public service have on policy making?"
- "Do you think that public servants should be accountable to the public?"
- "What are your own views on privatisation?"
- "To what extent to do you think that governments in Western Europe are really democratic?"
- "What contradictions do you see between the granting of civil rights and the maintenance of public order?"

KEY CONCEPTS

- Many companies have a specific selection policy, which can be discovered by examining their documentation.

- The management structure will determine, to a large extent, what the company's selection policy will be.

- The views of company founders have a profound influence on company selection policy.

- Modern employment equality legislation has forced panels to use more focused questions when interviewing job applicants.

7

Assessment Centre Selection

*The assessment centre approach is one in which poten-
tial employees are assessed for their suitability for a job
by groups of occupational psychologists and trained interviewers using a variety of selection procedures. Frequently, the interviewees are given structured exercises
and job sampling activities to complete. Their performance on these is assessed by senior managers from the
recruiting organisations.*

Potential job applicants are invited to attend a 1 or 2-day session in relation to the job for which they have applied. The procedure may involve a dinner, where the company representa-
tives mix freely with the job applicants, a series of aptitude tests,
a group interview, a one to one interview and an opportunity
for each candidate to express his/her views concerning some
topic which is given on the day of the interview.

Such assessment procedures are very demanding for interview candidates and it is vitally important for you to think out
your strategy well in advance.

- What are you going to talk about if you are asked to express
  an opinion?
- What slant are you going to take?
- How would you describe yourself in a 3-minute account?

Describing Yourself

There is no reason to be put out by such a request because, if
you think about it, there is no one you know more about than
yourself.

You should try to highlight your strengths and be ready with
an explanation of your weaknesses. It is sensible to admit that
you failed at certain things, but make sure you demonstrate how
you coped with such failure. Dealing with failure is regarded as
a positive virtue, whereas too much success can signify an

unwillingness to learn.

The guidelines that have already been given for answering questions should also be used in this instance. It is a good idea to try to list points if you are asked to speak off the cuff and to be definite about what you have to say. Remember, the interviewers are trying to assess what kind of person you are, rather than the amount of knowledge you have. Therefore, the way you respond is far more important than what you say. It is most unlikely that anyone is going to contradict you when you are giving a talk of this nature.

Likely Topics

- The state of the economy.
- How the company fits in with the industry in question.
- Strikes.
- Motivation.
- Management approaches.
- Sales strategies and others that are appropriate for the company in question.

Tips for Off the Cuff Speeches

When you are asked to speak off the cuff on a topic that you have not prepared you must immediately structure your response in such a way that you can have one section of the topic leading into another. This is not as difficult as it may seem.

1. Make a brief statement about the subject matter.
2. While you are making the statement internally prod yourself by asking questions such as why, what, when, how and where?
3. These questions should lead you to further statements concerning the topic and while making these you ought to be thinking of opposite statements as well as parallel ones to those you have made.
4. If at all possible use terms like firstly, secondly and thirdly because these will enable you to extend your topic as you continue.
5. Summarise what you have said in a few brief sentences.

Let us assume that you are asked to give a brief account of the state of the economy. A question of this nature will tend to put some candidates off entirely but if you merely make a very loose statement (such as "The economy is in a very poor state") you will have started and, to the questions that are mentioned above, you can answer by saying:

- because of the world recession (why);
- industrial output is down, agriculture is doing poorly, the rate of inflation is increasing and there is widespread unemployment (what);
- this recession began with the first of the oil crises or this recession is due to the overspending of the 1980s on armaments (when);
- the poor state of the economy is to be seen in the poor housing, unfunded hospitals, lack of confidence in financial circles (how).

While you are delivering the above material, perhaps hesitatingly, you could very easily and successfully have your mind focused on the opposite of the above statements, so that in the next section of your speech you could talk about the economy in a more positive way. You could say, for instance.

> *In many respects the economy is quite sound. After all, the rate of inflation is the lowest for many years and the massive growth that was occuring the public service in the 1960s has been halted. Many people are car owners today and it can be seen from the growth of leisure centres that people are no beginning to have more time off. This concentration on leisure is a very good sign of the economy really because firstly, it demonstrates that people have more money to spend, secondly, it increases the number of facilities available to tourists and, thirdly, it is good for the construction industry which is one of the best indicators of the state of the economy.*

The interviewers do not expect you to be absolutely familiar with the statistical data concerning the subject and they will tend to be very satisfied if you speak confidently about a narrow area. The interviewers are less interested in the content of what you say than in your manner of expression. They are anxious through such methods to assess your:

- resourcefulness;

- ability to deal with stress;
- communication skills;
- effect on others;
- general knowledge;
- ability to explore a topic.

Group Interviews and Group Dynamics

Assessment centre techniques are quite concerned with your re-actions in group situations and one of the great problems that interviewees have is that they get the feeling of being constantly under observation. It is better to ignore this aspect of the inter-action and to act in as natural a fashion as possible if you are to do yourself justice.

> *No matter how hard you try, you cannot make yourself into someone you are not. Therefore, it is better for you not to try. Your colleagues at the assessment centre will feel the very same as you do. There are certain guide-lines that you might follow in order to do your self justice at the assessment centre.*

How to Behave at Assessment Centres

- Don't put your colleagues down, no matter how much you are goaded into doing so.
- Speak positively rather than negatively about matters un-der discussion.
- Avoid complaining.
- Show a little knowledge but not so much as to sound over-confident.
- Make sure you interrupt from time to time and that you do it courteously.
- Preface your answers with statements such as "I feel" or "in my opinion" even when you are certain that you are right.
- Avoid too many gesticulations.
- Be careful not to let yourself slip into too relaxed a pose.

Influence of Assessment Centre Procedures

Quite a number of companies use assessment centre approaches when selecting employees. In their selection methods are included aptitude tests, group interviews, individual interviews and questionnaires.

Generally speaking, multinational corporations, large public companies, government departments and other organisations with extensive resources employ as wide a number of methods and techniques as possible when selecting employees. These organisations are very conscious of the fact that the interview is a highly subjective procedure and open to abuse.

If you are asked to participate in this type of selection procedure, you should use the same guidelines as mentioned above for assessment centres, as well as other relevant ones mentioned in this book.

KEY CONCEPTS

- Interviewers use a combination of many techniques during assessment centre sessions.

- The techniques that are used in assessment centre sessions are based on insights from the personnel and psychological fields.

- Many large companies adopt the same procedures as those used in assessment centre approaches.

8

Aptitude Tests

The number of applicants for jobs in recent years has lead to the construction of series of tests, which are used as screening devices for applicants before, or in conjunction with, the interview. The reasoning behind these tests is that employees need to have many other abilities, besides purely academic ones.

A great deal of research has been done on breaking down job tasks into their component parts so that essential aptitudes can be identified and included in sets of screeening tests. Generally speaking, aptitude tests can be divided into two categories:

1. verbal;
2. non-verbal.

The format of the questions in these categories is usually multiple choice and there is always only one answer.

Verbal Aptitude Tests

Verbal aptitude tests may range from an easy 5-minute vocabulary test, such as the PTI Verbal of the American Psychological Corporation (APC) aimed at industrial apprentices, to the Miller Analogies Test (APC) of about an hour's duration, used for screening applicants to graduate school. The latter are used for assessing well-educated applicants for professional and managerial jobs requiring at least a bachelor's degree. Aptitude tests that are classified as verbal tests include tests of logical reasoning, language usage and spelling. They are used as screening tests for banking, nursing, engineering, management, accountancy, personnel, insurance and army professions. They are also frequently used for screening apprentices and technicians.

There is a verbal component in all of these tests and the degree of reasoning required depends on the type and level of the position being applied for. These aptitude tests often take the form of sentence completion, word fluency, speed of association and reading comprehension. In particular, tests of reading comprehension have become increasingly important for predicting training and job performance in various jobs, such as chefs, repairmen and factory workers.

Some examples of the more important and, perhaps, more difficult aptitude tests are given below. If you wish to have a more detailed treatment you should consult books which deal with aptitude tests exclusively (see the Bibliography).

Logical Reasoning

Since logical reasoning abilities refer to seeing the relationships between different verbal concepts and being able to arrive at sensible conclusions from the given data, the testers have devised test items based on:

- analogues;
- synonyms and antonyms;
- odd-man-out questions;
- syllogisms;
- general verbal comprehension;
- verbal comprehension for technical jobs.

Analogues

Normally, the items are taken from everyday usage but they can be quite difficult to solve when the component parts of the items are arranged in unexpected ways. It is important for you, therefore, to familiarise yourself with basic concepts dealing with the above items in everyday life. The relationships between opposites (antonyms), such as black and white or night and day, are fairly easy to resolve, but those between more complex concepts can take some time to establish.

The following examples of analogues will illustrate how the relationships between a number of very simple verbal concepts can be made complex by rearranging them so that they are presented in an unusual manner.

1. **Clarity** is to **obscurity** as **modernity** is to **antiquity**.
2. **Clarity** is to **modernity** as **obscurity** is to **antiquity**.
3. **Obscurity** is to **clarity** as **antiquity** is to **modernity**.
4. **Modernity** is to **antiquity** as **clarity** is to **obscurity**.

If we study four words such as clarity, obscurity, modernity and antiquity, it is very easy to see that the first is the opposite of the second and the third is the opposite of the fourth. However, if the analogy that you are presented with is, "Clarity is to obscurity as modernity is to_____", it becomes quite difficult to find the fourth item. The above examples illustrate that there are at least four ways in which the relationships can be expressed.

Here are some further examples:

- Sky is to earth as ceiling is to_____.
- Day is to night as black is to_____.
- Cover is to book as _____ is to letter.
- Week is to day as_____is to month.

Answers: floor, white, envelope, year.

By changing the wording in any of the examples given above you can increase or decrease the degree of complexity. As indicated in the final chapter you should practise doing this mentally as part of your overall self-preparation for undertaking verbal reasoning aptitude tests. For example, if you change the first analogue to, "ceiling is to earth as sky is to_____" you will have a more difficult question to answer.

There can be many other variations of the above theme and candidates may find one particular format easier than another. The same kind of diversity can be created with all aptitude tests.

Synonyms and Antonyms

In the following examples of synonyms you are asked to indicate which word on the right (A, B, C, D or E) bears a similar relation to each of the two words on the left.

	A	B	C	D	E
sensible noise	sound	judgement	tone	silly	sensitive
dark heavy	night	unseen	weight	light	bright
chorus abstain	verse	averse	report	refrain	ignore
Answers: 1 (A), 2 (D), 3(D)					

Antonyms are opposites and questions are frequently expressed in a similar way to the examples of synonyms given above.

In the following example of antonyms, you are asked to pick out which word on the right is the opposite of the word on the left.

Devious kind, calm, clear, suave, honest.

Answer: *honest*

Odd-man-out Questions

Sometimes, the basis for the verbal reasoning tests is rather narrow. The answers to questions can depend as much on your general knowledge as on your verbal reasoning abilities. If you are asked to select the odd-man-out in a group of cities, your answer will depend on your level of general knowledge rather than on your logic. Therefore, when preparing for such tests, you should make sure that you are aware of all the possible ways in which these questions can be phrased.

In each of the following row of words, underline the word that is most different to the others.
- Beautiful, handsome, good-looking, pretty, kind.
- Horse, dog, cat, cow, fox.
- Sailed, ran, rode, flew, travelled.
- Fight, confront, argue, debate, reflect.
- Fix, cure, correct, repair, retrain.

Answers: *(a) kind; (b) fox; (c) travelled; (d) reflect; (e) retrain.*

Syllogisms

In these types of questions you are being tested for logical reasoning ability. You are given a number of facts and asked to make logical conclusions on the basis of the data given.

> *The Revenue Commissioners have raised some queries on the travelling expenses on my tax returns. I must provide an adequate explanation.*
>
> **Conclusion:**
> *Therefore, I must search for documentary support.*

*He failed his college entrance examination by a few marks. He
wants to go to college.*

Conclusion:
He must repeat the examination.

Logical reasoning can at first be practised with the above everyday types of examples and then turned into more technical or
commercial styles according to the intended career. It is a matter of looking for situations in which you can apply this pattern
of thought so that you exercise your mind and, as you practise,
you will find it increasingly easy.

While you may feel that it is easier and more satisfying for
you to obtain a book of aptitude tests and practise all the various types, there is no doubt that the amount you will learn from
trying to compose the tests yourself is enormous. Such self-preparation will condition you to be receptive when you undertake
the tests.

General Verbal Comprehension

Comprehension passages can be tested on the basis of multiple
choice items from which the candidate is asked to select or questions can be asked concerning the text. Comprehension questions may be very simple but if a speed dimension is introduced
into the tests they can be very difficult. This is precisely what
the selection boards tend to do and many candidates become
very frustrated when put under such pressure. Read the following passage and answer the questions at the end. Place a tick
after the answer you think is correct.

*Bridges must be built sufficiently strongly to support their own
weights and the volume of traffic that crosses them. They must be
able to resist the worst conditions of wind, flood and ice. In 1879
the Tay Railway Bridge in Scotland, which was designed years
before to be one of the longest wrought iron bridges in the world,
collapsed after only a year and a half of use. In an 80-mile an
hour gale, thirteen spars of the middle bridge were torn from
their piers of brick and stone. Then, in the darkness, a mail train
plunged from the bridge into the freezing waters below.*

*Even without the use of mortar, the Romans constructed some
powerful bridges. About twelve miles from the town of Nantes*

in France, they built a gigantic aqueduct, 155 feet high, over the River Garde. Built in 19BC, this structure rises in three tiers of arches, along the topmost one of which runs a channel for water. Today, it is possible to cross the aqueduct by walking along the passage made to supply water for the Romans and those whom they ruled.

1.   *Bridges must be:*
(a)   long;
(b)   heavy;
(c)   wide;
(d)   sturdy.

2.   *The piers of the Tay Railway Bridge were built of:*
(a)   brick and wrought-iron;
(b)   brick and stone;
(c)   wrought-iron and stone;
(d)   stone and mortar.

3.   *Why did the mail train plunge into the water?*
(a)   The tracks were broken.
(b)   It was blown into the water.
(c)   It was a very dark night.
(d)   The tracks were icy.

4.   *Aqueducts were built to carry:*
(a)   Romans;
(b)   trains;
(c)   water;
(d)   pedestrians.

5.   *How do you know that the Roman aqueduct was well built?*
(a)   It was built with mortar.
(b)   It had three tiers.
(c)   It still exists.
(d)   It was gigantic.

Answers: 1 (d), 2 (b), 3(a), 4 (c), 5 (c)

Verbal Comprehension for Technical Jobs

Practically all occupations require a certain level of verbal reasoning ability but a certain number of them require a higher level than others and you should pay particular attention to these. Since many employees eventually assume management or supervisory roles of one kind or another, a primary characteristic they will need is to be logical.

Verbal reasoning tests, therefore, will often be used in technical as well as in management-type interviews. The interview panels wish to know whether the candidate can see the relationship between different concepts, sift through the value of each one and finally formulate a reasonably acceptable answer to the question.

The positions where there is a strong emphasis on this aptitude include the positions of managing director, supervisor, solicitor, barrister, doctor, negotiator, personnel officer, bank official, police officer, psychologist, counsellor, politician, management accountant, production manager, marketing and sales manager, financial controller and many others. If you expect to obtain an aptitude test in any of these fields of activity you can be reasonably sure that a verbal reasoning aptitude will be given.

In many cases the items for reading comprehension tests are taken from the training manuals that are used on the job and are, therefore, assumed to have a high level of validity. It has been found recently that a high level of verbal comprehension is as important for technical jobs as it is for jobs in law or personnel. To be able to read manuals accurately and with comprehension is a most important aptitude for people working in technical areas.

The passage given below is based on data included in manuals related to sound engineering and computers. It does not require a vast grasp of mathematics or physics to work through the questions. Such knowledge is part of the kind of interview knowledge that applicants for sound engineering or computer positions would need to have. The example is given for the purpose of emphasising that you may be given such types of tests in screening sessions for technical or technological positions. If a speed element is introduced into these tests, they can be very exacting indeed.

Read the passage below and answer the comprehension questions underneath it.

Data Protocols

Different types of (i)_____exist for the RS 232C se-
rial interface depending on the computer manufacturer.
Check your computer (ii)_____for which of the following protocols your computer uses: X ON/X OFF or
DC1/DC3, DTR, RC, ETX/ACK
     These protocols are provided to protect overflow of the
print data receive (iii)_____when the interface data
transmission speed is faster than the buffer data print
speed. Therefore, the printer uses specific character
(iv)_____ or an interface signal for each protocol to
inform the (v)_____ of the buffer status.

Answers:
(i) protocols, (ii) manual, (iii) buffer, (iv) codes, (v) host

A test on the above passage could also be given on the basis of a
direct comprehension test to discover whether you are likely to
understand how the printer works.

Non-verbal AptitudeTests

Under the heading of non-verbal tests are included numerical
and spatial tests. The former are easy enough to comprehend,
while the latter assess your ability to see things in three dimensions, as well as your aesthetic and perceptual sense. Non-verbal tests can be given in many different ways, but the basic principles are always the same. What the testers are trying to find
out is whether, in the case of numeracy, you have the ability to
add and subtract, to multiply and divide. In the case of the spatial tests, they seek to establish whether or not you understand
the differences between triangles and squares, circles and el-
lipses, parallelograms and rectangles. A number of examples
are given below and, as in the case of the verbal tests outlined
earlier, the treatment is not intended to be exhaustive but rather
an introduction to the subject.

Numerical Ability Tests

In the case of these tests it is possible to compile suitable tests
from your own day to day life. Everyone has to acquire a certain
level of numerical competence in order to survive in Western

society. Furthermore, many of the items that are included in numerical tests use a similar type of reasoning to that which is used in the verbal tests earlier in this chapter. Here are a few examples to illustrate this point. (Answers are given at the end of the chapter.)

Odd-man-out Questions

Underline the odd-man-out in the following questions.
(a)   25, 169, 49, 81, 35.
(b)   0.05, 0.01, 0.5, 1.3, 0.001.
(c)   27, 81, 71, 243, 729.
(d)   5, 7, 9, 17, 23, 37.
(e)   22, 34, 48, 14, 53.

Series Tests

What number comes next in each of the following?
(a)   1, 2, 4, 8, 16, _____.
(b)   3, 3, 7, 7, 11, _____.
(c)   130, 118, 107, 97, 88, _____.
(d)   2, 3, 5, 8, 12, _____.

Mental Arithmetic Tests

Apart from the above kinds of numerical ability tests, there are other tests of speed and accuracy in mental arithmetic which are worth knowing. They are the kinds of questions frequently covered in primary schools. This does not mean that they are simple and, when a speed element is introduced, they become even more difficult.
1.   If I invest £1,000 for one year at 1.5% interest what total amount of money will I have at the end of the year?
2.   What is 33.33% of 963?
3.   Divide 0.75 into 2.25
4.   What is half of a half?

These should be practised to enable you to perform well when under pressure.

Obviously, if you compute the above questions with pen and paper, it could take a good deal of time. If you do them in your head you will be able to take short cuts.

When preparing for numerical aptitude tests you should base your computations on the world around you because it is from this world that the testers draw the questions.

Examples

1.   If I have a tax allowance of £6,000 on a salary of £20,000,
      the amount of tax I will have to pay (if the rate is 25%) is
      £20,000 - £6,000 = £14,000; divided by 4 (25%) = £3,500

2.   The amount of VAT I will have to pay on a bill of £250 if
      the rate is 7% = 2.5 X 7 = £17.50 (the shortest way to cal-
      culate in this case is to put 7 over 100 and multiply by 250
      which will give the above figures).

3.   If I obtain a reduction of £37 on a bill of £4,000, what
      percentage reduction have I been given?

$$\frac{37}{4,000} \text{ X } \frac{100}{1} = \frac{37}{40} = 9.25\%$$

It is clear from the above examples that you may use a combination of subtraction, addition, multiplication, division, decimals,
fractions and percentages to answer such questions. Many of
the numerical questions deal with numbers from one to twelve
and if you are fully familiar with all possible operations that can
be carried out with these numbers you should be able to perform very well.

Look at the following numbers:

   4, 9, 16, 25, 36, 49, 64, 81, 100, 121, 124.

They are the square root of numbers from two to twelve and if
you are asked to obtain the square root of any of these you should
not have any problem identifying them.

The same applies to cube roots:

   8, 27, 64, 125, 216, 343, 256, 729, 1,000, 1,331, 1,488.

If you concentrate on improving your performance in mental
arithmetic there is no doubt that you will perform well in numerical ability tests. So, when you are given change, or when
the groceries are being recorded at the checkout, always calculate your bill mentally. Such activity will make you sharp in

numerical ability aptitude tests. Dispense with your calculator for simple problems and only use it when absolutely necessary.

Numerical Analogues

Analogues are processes of reasoning from parallel cases. To understand how to complete them you must discover the underlying pattern on which they are based. You will be given an example and you must study it to see the pattern you will be expected to follow in order to get the answer to the test given.

Test your ability by studying the following examples.

Instructions: *Fill in the missing numbers where the questions marks appear.* (Answers are given at the end of the chapter.)

Example 1

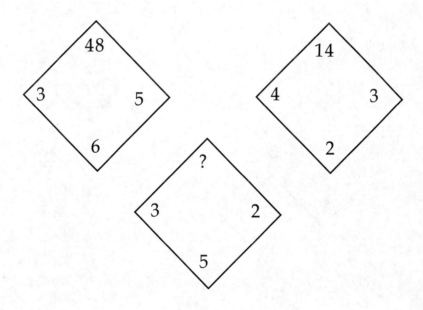

Example 2

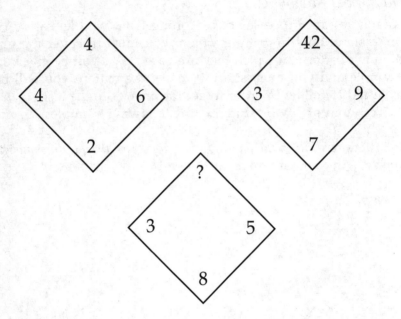

Example 3

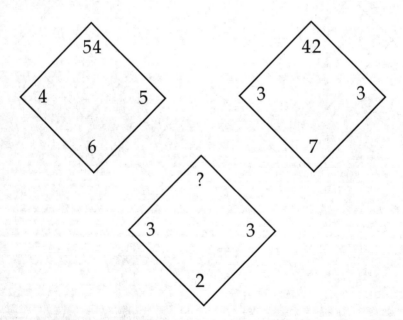

Space Relations Tests

It is felt by many people that these are the most difficult tests of all. They test your understanding of figures in three dimensions, your visual and spatial sense and your ability to grasp the concepts that are associated with buildings, constructions, patterns, engineering, computing and many other activities. In these tests the amount of self-preparation can be substantial. We are living in an environment where there are squares, rectangles, circles, parallelograms and other shapes all around us.

The following is a mixed set of space relations examples. There are many more types but the same principles of visual perception and space relations aptitude applies to them all.

Example 1

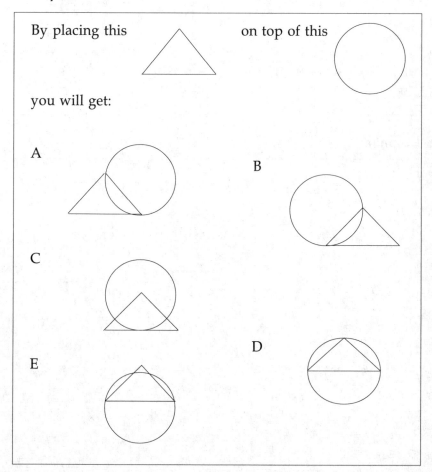

Example 2

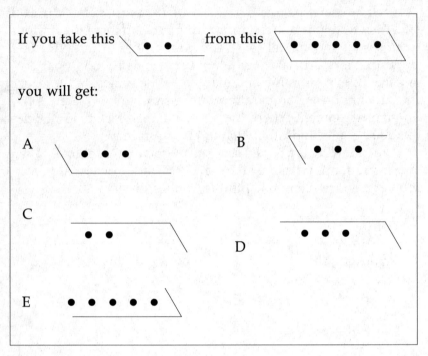

Example 3

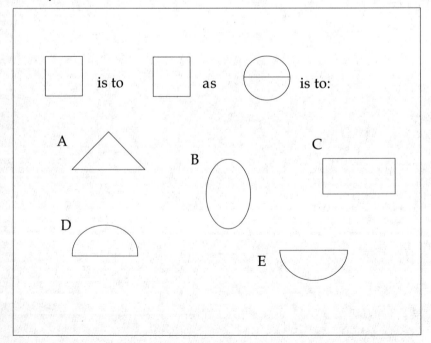

Answers to the Numerical Ability Tests in this Chapter

Take particular note of the reasons that are given for these answers so that you will be able to practise many other similar examples yourself.

Odd-man-out

(a)   35
    All the other numbers are squares of numbers.
(b)   1.3
    All the other numbers are below 1.00.
(c)   71
    All other numbers are multiples of 3.
(d)   9
    This is a prime number, all the others are whole numbers.
(e)   53
    All the other numbers are even.

Series

(a)   32
    The next number is double the one before it on each occasion.
(b)   11
    Each number is put down twice.
(c)   80
    The difference between each number and the one following it decreases by one each time from 12 to 11, to 10 and so on.
(d)   17
    The difference between each number and the one following it increases by one each time from 1 to 2 to 3 and so on.

Mental Arithmatic

1.   1,015
    The first question often elicits an answer of £1,500 when the decimal point is not moved far enough.
2.   321
    The best way of doing (2) is to turn the percentage into the fraction 1/3 and, therefore, divide by 3.

3.   3
4.   ¼.

Numerical Analogues

1.   25
      Add the middle numbers and multiply the result by the
      bottom number.
2.   16
      Subtract the middle-left number from the middle-right
      number and multiply the result by the bottom number.
3:    12
      Add the middle numbers and multiply the result by the
      bottom number.

Space Relations Tests

1.   D
2.   D
3.   E

In the final chapter you will find further tips for dealing with
aptitude tests when you read how you can train yourself how
to cope with them.

KEY CONCEPTS

- Aptitude tests are based on certain crucial dimensions which can be established by close observation.

- The types of aptitude tests given by employers are related to the skills required on the job – logical reasoning for management, mechanical reasoning for engineers, numeracy for accountants.

- The items for aptitude tests are normally taken from your everyday environment.

9

CVs and Covering Letters

This chapter deals with the crucial matter of written presentation of materials to interview panels. This is an area you should not neglect. You won't be called for interview at all if you don't see to this matter in the first instance. Before dealing with these concerns, however, look at the three sample envelopes, the covering letter and the CV in the following pages. Evaluate them under the following headings: visual impact, what they tell you about the job applicant, content, layout and overall impression.

Samples

1.

> Mr. Murray,
>   Managing Director,
>   Kitchen Appliances,
>   15 Pappan's Drive,
>   Surrey

2.

> Secretary,
> Pfizer Chemical Corporation,
>   15, Commons Road,
>   Swansea

3.

> Personnel Manager
>   Smith's Industries
>   14 Merchant's Quay
>   Liverpool

The impression created by the above job applicants is that they are careless in their approach to the interview. The address is badly laid out on all envelopes, the title 'Human Resources Manager' should be used rather than 'Secretary' on number 2 and there should be commas after each line of the address in number 3. The stamp is upside down in one of them, crooked in another one and in the wrong place in the third. The name for one of the companies is spelled incorrectly and the letters 'Ltd' should be put after another. The applicants may reach the interview but when it comes to a competitive choice concerning who is going to be selected for a position, interviewers tend to have a great deal of respect for clarity, neatness and order.

Tips for Addressing the Envelope

- Always use a long white 6″ X 4″ envelope for a covering letter plus standard application form.
- Use a 12″ X 5″ brown envelope when sending a CV and covering letter.
- Place the stamp squarely on the top right hand side of the envelope.
- Make sure you have the same margin all round.
- Keep your writing as straight as possible and trace your name through a lined page if necessary.
- Use the correct title given in the advertisement, i.e. Personnel Manager, Secretary or Managing Director.
- If possible, obtain and use the name of the person you are writing to by telephoning the organisation for the information.
- Check the telephone directory to make sure you have the correct company name and address.
- Allow a separate line for each section of the address: the person's name on the first line, the title on the second, the company on the third, the street number and name on the fourth, the county on the fifth and the country (where necessary) on the sixth.
- Make sure there are no smudges, finger marks or other marks on the envelope.
- Normally, companies expect that the envelope will be addressed in your own handwriting.
- Make sure your envelope doesn't look like an ordinary circular in case it ends up, unopened, in the wastepaper basket.

The Covering Letter

Many job applicants neglect to write a covering letter when applying for positions. They feel that the completed application form is sufficient. This is a mistake because they are missing an opportunity which gives great scope to highlight their unique features.

Tips for writing a Covering Letter

- The covering letter must be brief and to the point, but it can make provision for the inclusion of a sentence or two which differentiates you from all other applicants.
- Put the address of the person to whom you are writing on the left-hand side of the page and your own address on the right-hand side.
- It is important that you have the proper name and title of the person to whom you are writing. After your opening salutation you refer to where you first learned about the position in question.
- Phraseology, such as "with reference to the position which you advertised" or "I would like to apply for the position", ought to be used.
- Your next paragraph may refer to some unique characteristic about you that differentiates you from other applicants.

You might make statements such as: "I feel I am particularly suitable for a position as cashier because of my position as treasurer for the choral society while at university" or, "I acted as PRO for the debating society and I feel the special skills which I acquired in that position prepared me well for a position in personnel." It will be up to you to devise sentences which will help you to sell yourself to the company.

The next paragraph will refer to the documents which you are enclosing for the perusal of the personnel manager and the last paragraph will state the expectation that you will hear from the company again. Some sample letters are given below.

A covering letter should be written on a blank A4 page, should never exceed one page and should be dated. It is a good idea to have the same border all round and to have a symmetry between your address, the address of the person you are writing to and your signature at the end of the letter.

Sample Covering Letters

13, St. George's Terrace,
Crosshaven,
Co. Cork,
Ireland

Mr. W.Keenan,
Personnel Manager,
Adztech Project Management,
14, Strand Street,
Blackpool,
UK

28th January 1999

Dear Mr. Keenan,

I wish to apply for the position of project officer with your company which was advertised in the Yorkshire Post last Saturday, 23rd January.

You will find enclosed my CV which details the experience I have acquired from participating in management-type activities at a second level school and from a major research project at the National Micro-electronics Centre, Cork, Ireland.

From involvement in the above activities, as well as from my academic attainment, I know I have the ability to perform to a high standard in the kinds of engineering projects which your company undertakes.

I would appreciate an answer as soon as is convenient for you. You may telephone me at Cork (00353)21-22000 or fax me at (00353)21-22444.

I look forward to hearing from you.

Yours sincerely,

John Egey

"St. Jude's" Redemption Road,
Wilton,
Birmingham

Secretary,
Hertz and Hyland,
Chartered Accountants,
31, Blackfriars Street,
Nottingham

21st January 1999

Dear Sir,

I am taking the liberty of circularising your company with my CV because I feel you may wish to take on a trainee accountant.

Your name was listed in the GET Directory as a company that has a number of vacancies annually.

The description of your company in the above directory stated that you were particularly interested in employing people who had a working knowledge of VAT rates, property tax and liquidation procedures. While I do not have experience in all of these areas, dealing with the VAT returns for the family business has given me an insight into what is required when negotiating with the Inland Revenue.

Should you wish to have more information concerning my background and experience, I would be very pleased indeed to have the opportunity of talking to you.

I trust that you find my CV of some interest and I look forward to hearing from you should a vacancy arise.

Yours sincerely,

James Bruff

The Curriculum Vitae

The CV is a special kind of document requiring a great deal of thought and care if it is to have the impact you desire.

Essentials

Your name, address, age, nationality and telephone number should be included at the beginning of the CV. Your telephone number or the telephone number of a contact should be given. Many companies today are too busy to write letters and they will telephone people at a moment's notice if a vacancy arises in an unexpected way. If you have not given a telephone number where you can be contacted you may be limiting your chances. If you have access to a fax, include the number.

Employment Record

The next area that needs to be mentioned in your CV is your employment record. You must be quite explicit in this regard and you should not undersell or oversell yourself. It is far better to identify specific functions that you have had, giving the relevant dates and companies, than to list your employment record as one mass of information. When you separate out the functions which you have performed you create a very clear impression that you understand what you are doing and that you would be an asset to the company.

In cases where the work may seem of a trivial nature to you it is vital not to make light of your experience. If you have spent some time working in a bar, for instance, and if you were given responsibility from time to time you must state this in an explicit way. It implies that you were trusted, that you had the ability to take charge and that you understand what accountability means.

In particular, if there were any elements of management in the position you should try to isolate the essential dimensions and specify them. You may have been working on a farm picking potatoes for the summer and the farmer may have put you in charge of a small group of people for the purpose of co-ordinating the work. You should state that you had acquired a certain level of skill in management and co-ordination of tasks since the opportunity is afforded to you in your CV. It is customary to start with your most recent work experience and go back over your record year by year.

Do not put anything down in this section that is unclear, because potential employers are anxious to know whether your experiences will be useful in the work that they have for you. If you make a statement such as "I was operating a computer workstation" you tell the potential employer nothing worthwhile, but what you do indicate, through your lack of explanation, is that you have very little understanding of teamwork.

Potential job applicants must realise where their work fits in the general pattern of things. It is far better to specify in a short sentence exactly what you were doing. You can then leave it to the employer to decide whether he/she wants you or not. Many job applicants do not know the relevance of the jobs at which they were working. They fail to see the relationship between what they were doing and the firm or industry in which they were working. It is important to think about these matters and to put down what the work experience entailed in a succinct sentence or two.

Educational Background

The most recent educational achievements should be given first. Outline results in tabular form. Highlight any distinctions or credits you obtained. Isolate the subject areas that you covered. Make particular reference to facets of such subjects that seem to be relevant to the job for which you are applying.

If you are applying for a job as an actuary with an insurance company, for instance, highlight your results in mathematics, if they were good. On the other hand, if you are applying for a position in personnel and you did courses in psychology you ought to give special mention to this subject, even if you did it to first-year level only while in college.

Remember that the employer is anxious to see how you can fit into the team he has already working for him. He will not have the time nor the expertise to see how the subjects you are listing may be useful to him. It is your business to present your expertise in the best possible light.

If you feel that you need to put in all your individual results, because of the nature of the job for which you are applying, you might consider putting them on a separate sheet and confine the data in the CV to the principal headings. In any case, your CV should not extend to more than three pages. Even though you ought to personalise the CV by using the first person from time to time, you must be extremely careful not to present an auto-biographical account which gives the impression that you have little more to learn.

Interests and Hobbies

Formerly, this section of a CV was merely a catalogue of the kinds of games that people played but, in recent years, a great deal of diversity has crept into people's leisure-time activities. In the case of interests and hobbies you should never assume that what you do is not of interest, even if the activities are different to those of everyone else. Your interests may be in photography, reading or music, football, squash or bridge, films or tennis. It does not really matter, because the fact that you are interested in something means that you can be enthusiastic and it may be possible to turn your enthusiasm for your hobby or interest into enthusiasm for the firm.

It is felt by employers that the job applicant who is interested in the world around him/her is also very likely to be interested in working hard. Therefore, when you are filling this section of your CV, you should give careful thought to what you are go-ing to write down. It would be extremely beneficial for you to indicate in some way how your involvement helps to develop your personality.

When speaking of games you might say that you play them for relaxation purposes and if you are referring to reading, mu-sic or photography it might be useful to mention some successes you have had, clubs you have joined or other group activities that they have lead to. In other words, you try to draw as much positive significance as possible out of your interests so that the interviewer will be able to get an insight into the kind of person you are.

If you are asked to discuss your interests in the interview it-self, you are being provided with a golden opportunity to talk about something in which you have a high level of expertise. Be prepared, so you can make the best of it.

The Wordprocessor

In the matter of CV layout, one of the most significant develop-ments in modern times has been the use of the wordprocessor. At its simplest, the wordprocessor is just a glorified typewriter because it does exactly the same job. You can type letters and application forms just as you used to do with the typewriter. However, there are some very significant differences. The letters you type can be reproduced as originals each time with very little effort. In other words you can vary the headings and re-print the same application form over and over again. Furthermore, you can vary the type, giving bold headings or italics for topics you want to emphasise. Anyone who has used a word-processor will know its capacity for the purpose of producing very impressive looking CVs.

Furthermore, you can vary the orientation of your CV as you move from vacancy to vacancy. At one stage you may wish to emphasise the work experience you had when you were working with a multinational company in Germany. At another stage you may feel that you should delete this matter and focus instead on certain hobbies or interests that you have. The clip board will enable you to move material rapidly from one CV to another. Furthermore, the delete facility in the wordprocessor will enable you to change the tone of covering letters so that you draw attention to areas in your CV that refer directly to the job on offer. The fact that you can present the material in bulleted points will enable you to give your document a very polished appearance. But, what do you to if you have no competence at all in this area? How do you manage if you are depending on others to type up your CV? The following guidelines should enable you to steer your way through the matter in such a manner that you can ensure that you are getting the best possible return for money which you may need to give to someone or some organisation to type your CV for you.

Do
- Insist on your wordprocessing person varying the size of the typescript.
- Keep in mind that the typescript can vary in size from 10 point size upwards.
- The words "curriculum vitae" should be the largest heading in the CV and no other heading should be of the same size (possibly at 18 or 20 point size).
- Headings such as 'education', 'work experience' as well as 'interests and hobbies' should be 14 or 16 point size.

- Examination results should be laid out in tabular form and can be arranged in two columns rather than one.
- The text of the CV should be justified which means that the right-hand side is aligned.
- Read the CV for spelling errors because it is sometimes rather difficult to pick out spelling errors in a piece of wordprocessed text.
- Watch out for instances where the spell check confirms that a spelling is right but it is wrong in fact, i.e the spell check will not identify a word as wrong if the way you have spelt it is the way it can be spelt in the dictionary, e.g synonyms, their and there or if you inadvertently type 'then' instead of 'the'.

Evaluating Information Supplied by Applicants

How you are Judged

- The information you put into a CV is regarded as being of a special kind because it can demonstrate, to a large extent, how you organise your own world.
- From the manner in which the envelope and covering letter are laid out, to the referees that are selected, the perceptive interviewer can glean a great deal.
- What is left out of the CV is often considered to be as important as what is put in.
- The colour or complexion that the job applicant gives to the information that is included provides vital clues to his/her personality.
- When the information in the CV is compared and contrasted with answers given to questions in the interview itself, a complete picture of the candidate begins to unfold.
- Job applicants should always make a photocopy of the documents which they have sent to interview panels because it is difficult to be certain what you have said after a period of time. It is also a good idea to bring that copy to the interview, in case the original has been mislaid.
- Interview panels often use your CV as a guide when asking questions. Therefore, it is most important to be consistent in your answers and not to be evasive regarding areas where

you think you show a certain weakness.

- If you did poorly in a particular subject and the interviewer refers to this, there is no need for you to be defensive. You should merely admit it, briefly explain why and wait for the next question.
- Interviewers are more often interested in gauging your ability to cope with failure than they are in excuses or explanations which you might try to give.
- You will be evaluated on the basis of your academic results, your work or educational experiences and how consistent a personality you seem to have.
- The fact that you dropped certain subjects that seem to be relevant to the job may be one of the deciding factors in your not being called for a certain interview. However, if you are able to give an acceptable reason for taking the course of action such a decision may be looked on in a positive way.

In the following pages you are given examples of CVs. The sample given under (A) for a poorly thought out CV for an academic under-achiever shows how it will look if only the bare facts are given, whereas the sample given under (B) for a well thought out CV will make a greater impression. In the latter case the sample job applicant derives maximum benefit from life experiences in order to increase his/her chances of being selected for a position, despite a rather average academic background. These CVs are followed by an example for a high achiever.

A   **A Poorly Thought Out CV for an Academic Under-achiever**

Name and Address J. Murphy, 17, Orchard Road, Dublin.

[Full name and address should always be given as in (B) below.]

Date of Birth   27-3-1968

[Using words as in (B) rather than figures reduces skimpiness.]

Employment Record

1995-1998   Shop assistant in a pottery factory shop.

[No matter what work you undertake close examination of the activities involved, as is carried out in (B), will enable you to demonstrate that you are self aware.]

1990-1995   Worked on a building site in England.

[Selection boards often decide that a person who understands the component parts of simple task can be trusted with greater ones. Sample (B) demonstrates this awareness.]

1985-1990   Barman.

[By clarifying what the barwork entailed, as is done in (B), you will be able to convince the selection board that you have excellent interpersonal skills.]

1973-1978   Newtown Primay School

Examinations

1983 Junior Certificate

English	(Pass)
French	(Pass)
Technical Drawing	(Pass)
Science	(Pass)
History	(Pass)
Geography	(Pass)
Mathematics	(Pass)

[While the above statement of results may be the actual standard of the certificate which you obtained, it would be better to put down the actual grades which you received, as is done in sample (B). You must present yourself in the best possible light and it is the employer's responsibility to establish what the relevance of the various grades is.]

1985 Leaving Certificate Examination

English	D	(Pass)
French	D	(Pass)
Economics	C	(Pass)
Mathematics	D	(Pass)
Physics	D	(Pass)
Technical Drawing	D	(Pass)
Chemistry	E	(Fail)

[You should keep the comments in relation to the Junior Certificate Examination above in mind here also. In the case of failed subjects it may be better not to include them at the CV stage but to talk about them during the interview if you are called. If the rest of the CV demonstrates attention to detail and higher performance at work related activities, academic failure may not be frowned on so much.]

Hobbies and Interests   Soccer, reading and chess

[This reply tells the selection boards very little about what you gained from such activities. You should elaborate a little about these, as is done in sample (B), in order to show your self awareness.]

References   Rev. J. James,
                            Rector,
                            Eyre Paris,
                            Sligo,
                            Ireland

                            The Principal,
                            St. Andrew's Secondary School,
                            Galway,
                            Ireland

B   A Well Thought Out CV for an Academic Under-achiever

Name and Address   Mr. John Murphy,
12, Orchard Road,
Dublin 2

**Contact Telephone
Number**   01-333 3333

Date of Birth   27th March 1968

Employment Record
1995-1998   Assistant in pottery with responsibility for sales, ordering and receipts. I took charge of the premises whenever the manager was away on business.
Skills acquired
The ability to deal with difficult customers, to accept responsibility and to delegate specific tasks to others.

1990-1995   Working on a building site in England.
(i) Two year's experience in acting as carpenter's mate.
(ii) Three year's experience as general builder's labourer with responsibility for mixing cement, cleaning the mixer, repairing equipment and taking order dockets to the hardware stores.
Skills acquired
The ability to take orders, to see that work is completed and to undertake building activities such as tilling, plastering, decorating, as well as these practical skills, I learned how business operates.

1985-1990   Barwork with responsibility for customer satisfaction, cash sales and orders. I was given total charge of the bar from time to time.
Skills acquired
Experience in dealing with the public and difficult customers.

Education Record

First Level

1973-1978   Newtown Primary School,
                 George's Square,
                 Galway,
                 Ireland
                 Telephone number: 091-11111.

Second Level

1979-1983   St. Andrews Secondary School,
                 Galway,
                 Ireland
                 Telephone 091-222222

Examinations: 1983

Intercert	(Pass)	Mathematics	(Pass)
Irish	(Pass)	History	(Pass)
Science	(Pass)	Geography	(Pass)
English	(Pass)		

Hobbies and Interests

I have been captain of the school soccer team on a number of occasions. I get a lot of satisfaction from reading features on the newspapers and I find the occasional game of pool or chess very relaxing.

References

Mr. Stepehen Geary,	Mr. Jack Hardiman,
The Potter's Shlop,	The Principal,
Napoleon Square,	St Andrew's Secondary
Patrick Street,	School,
Glasgow	Galway,
Scotland	Ireland
Telephone:	*Telephone:*
00-44-141-456234	*091-222222*

C   Sample CV of a High Academic Achiever

Name	John Example.
Address	10 Enterprise Street
	Cork.
Date of Birth	8 June 1968
Nationality	Irish
Telephone	Cork 021-22000
Fax	Cork 021-22444

EDUCATION

First Level	**1973-1978**
	School of Junior Education,
	Blackrock,
	Cork
Second Level	**1979-1983**
	School of Senior Education,
	Dalkey,
	Co. Dublin

Examinations

Senior Secondary Examinations (1985)

Subjects **	Leaving Cert Grade	Matriculation Cert* Grade
Irish	B	A
English	B	C
Mathematics	B	A
French	A	B
Chemistry	B	A
Physics	B	B
Economics	B	***

*   National University of Ireland Entrance Examination.
**   All Honours subjects.
***   No paper available in this subject.

Obtained 28 points out of a maximum of 32 in the above examinations.

Third Level Course

Bachelor of Electrical and Microelectronic Engineering,
University College Galway,
Ireland

First Year (1986)   **First Class Honours**
Examination Distinction   Award of College Scholar.
Subjects
Maths, Computer Science (Pascal) Maths-Physics, Physics, Chemistry, Electrical Engineering.

Second Year (1987)   **First Class Honours**
Examination Distinctions   Award of College Scholar and selected by the Department of Computer Science to tutor Joint Honours students in Fortran.
Subjects
Thermodynamics, Electronics, Electronic Materials and Devices, Power Engineering, Fortran and Numerical Analysis, Mathematics, Maths Physics, Spanish.

Third Year (1988)   **First Class Honours**
Examination Distinctions   Award of College Scholar.
Subjects
Solid-state Electronics, Circuit Analysis, Electrical Machines, Assembly Language, Computer Architecture and Design, Control Engineering, Mechanical Engineering, Maths, Electro-magnetic Field Theory.

Fourth Year (1989)   **First Class Honours**
Examination Distinctions   Award of College Scholar
Subjects
Microelectronics, Digital Electronics, Digital Signal Processing, Power Electronics, Telecommunications, Opto-electronics, Control Engineering, Applied Mathematics.

HOBBIES AND INTERESTS
Athletics, second place in All Ireland Relay Competitions 1986. Rugby, winger for Cork squad in 1985.
Debating, member of winning Junior Chamber of Commerce team in 1986. Chess.

REFEREES

Mr. James Example,	Mr. Peter Smythe,
Manager,	Principal,
S.I.L.C,	School of Senior Education,
Prospect Row,	Dalkey,
Cork.	Co. Dublin
Telephone (021) 276871	Telephone (01) 5437901

SIGNED 25th January 1999

The Electronic CV and the World Wide Web

In the past number of years there have been great strides in the areas of internet and web technology. There are very few important companies today who do not have a presence on the World Wide Web. Furthermore, recruitment agencies and the HRM departments of companies use their web sites to advertise the vacancies that they have. The very nature of the internet enables companies and organisations to let the world know what vacancies they have, the job requirements and the general thrust of the companies. This information can be made available to job applicants very rapidly. Therefore, such applicants have a head start if they are aware of the manner in which the web can be used for the promotion of the job searchers interests.

The following step by step account of the procedures that you need to adopt in order to convert your general CV into an electronic one are given so that you will be able to ensure that you make potential employers. The Lankford HRM web site is being given as an example of the potential this medium has for the intending job applicant.

Accessing the System

- From your web browser open the following URL: http://www.silk.ie/LankfordHRM.
  [This is done by going to the "File" menu of your browser, selecting "Open" and typing: http://www.silk.ie/LankfordHRM.]
- Carefully study the other CVs on the Lankford HRM site to see how best you can present yours.
- Send an e-mail to the LankfordHRM, lankfordc@yahoo.com, in order to establish what is the best way to proceed and to get an opinion about your CV.
- Send your CV in Word 6.0 format. It would also be helpful to send your CV as plain text or ASCII format as is often referred to.

Promoting Yourself on the World Wide Web

Due to the fact that there are thousands of CVs already on the internet you need to present yours in a way that stands out. If it is all continuous text it is unlikely to be read by anyone. On the other hand if it is bulleted and highlighted in the same way as the CVs in this chapter you may have a good possibility of it being noticed Keep the following pointers in mind concerning your electronic CV.

- You are the person who will need to keep an eye on the vacancies in order to establish whether you have the characteristics and the qualifications that are required.
- Just as in everyday life nothing will happen on the internet unless you make it happen.
- You will need to be proactive about your CV to the extent that you will need to send it to all employers as soon as vacancies arise.
- In order to cater for vacancies that arise from time to time you will need to have a covering letter that you can adapt rapidly to new situations.
- Due to the fact that the whole emphasis in internet and web technology is on speed and change you will need to respond immediately to any enquiries that you obtain. If you don't do this others will lose interest in you.
- Ensure that you have an e-mail address on your CV so that employers and recruitment agencies can respond to your needs.
- Ensure that any bullet points that you are using in the CV will come up properly in copies that may be printed by interested parties.
- Even though many services on the internet are free, it may be in your interest to pay someone who is advertising his or her internet CV promotion services because of the amount of time it saves you.
- Take great care in regard to the pagination in order to ensure that your CV will come out of a computer in a clear, attractive and logical way – there is a great danger that words will run into one another if you don't make sure that the spacing between words, sentences and pages is adequate.

Key Concepts

- It is an employer's market and your initial correspondence is your only calling card and your first introduction to the company.

- Monitor what you put on your CV carefully. It is likely to be queried. Be prepared to answer questions on it.

- Do not leave significant gaps in your life's history. Do not draw unnecessary attention to weaknesses in subject areas.

- Give a telephone number where you can be contacted. Identify important skills you acquired from working.

- Give names of referees, but make sure you have their permission to use them.

- Give examples of your strengths or aptitudes and how you have used them.

- Make sure that the CV is properly typed with all the appropriate headings.

- Try to make extensive and intensive use of all the modern technologies that are available to you for enhancing your CV and presentation.

10

DIY Interview Training

Just as is the case with physical exercise, or learning a musical instrument, there are certain steps that can be taken in order to ensure excellent performance in the employment interview. You can learn these steps through what I have called DIY interview training.

You don't have to be an expert in training to accept that you have to practise a skill if you want to reach perfection. Many of the guidelines and suggestions in this book refer to such skills and how to acquire them. This chapter focuses on how you may bring all these guidelines and suggestions to bear on your DIY training scheme, so that you will get the most out of yourself and reach your goal, which is obtaining a job.

The DIY training programme proposed here is a hands-on training programme which focuses on maximum participation by you in the learning process. A training programme is said to be effective only to the extent that the trainee actively participates in what is happening. Such a programme has got to include long, medium and short-term preparation. It must be research-based if it is to be effective. Above all, it has got to be self-directed and hands-on in nature, i.e. you must do it yourself. The most important ingredient is your active and willing co-operation at all stages.

Essential techniques that have been developed in the area of hands-on training are the techniques of role-playing, simulation, feedback, modelling and assertiveness. All of these techniques have got to be practised internally and externally by you. The DIY strategies for success in the employment interview are dealt with under three distinct headings, which can also be applied to aptitudes, dealt with later in this chapter.

1. The research stage.
2. The self-preparation stage.
3. Interactive training techniques.

1.   Research Stage

The sources of information regarding the company to which you are applying and the interview procedures they adopt are many and varied. Apart from those already listed in Chapter 3, there are other ways you can obtain further information from the following.

- In-house journals which the company publishes.
- Trade union reports from employees who are working in the company.
- Suppliers of services and goods to the company.
- Company employees.
- Company annual reports.
- The registry of businesses.
- Industrial development authorities, particularly if the government has given the company grants.
- Business and finance journals.
- Newspaper articles and cuttings which can, normally, be accessed in the local public library.
- Books written about the company or its founders.
- The advertisements through which the company advertises its products or services. These will enlighten you regarding recruitment policy.

For information on the industry look at the following.

- Industrial statistics from the Central Statistics Office.
- Business pages of newspapers.
- Workers in the industry.
- Stock exchange information if it is a quoted public company.
- Competitors.
- Video materials.
- Careers directories such as GET, GO and others available in libraries.

For the job itself examine the following.

- Career leaflets and a careers encyclopedia.

- Trade union meetings.
- Workers in the job.
- Books by people who are in the job.
- Open University courses.
- Newspaper and television reports.
- The requirements indicated in the job advertisements.

For information on the qualifications required look at the following.

- Careers encyclopedias.
- Directories of qualifications.
- Prospectuses of individual colleges.
- Directories of recognised qualifications.
- Always check the qualifications required for a job by telephoning the relevant institute.

For information on the interview itself look at the following.

- Sample interviews in books, videos, tapes and on television.
- The advertisement itself may say that the company is looking for people with such characteristics as initiative, leadership, motivation and self confidence, along with skills in certain areas. The interview panel may ask questions that they feel will throw some light on these matters.
- Discussions with employees of the firm in question.
- Articles in newspapers which indicate new approaches being adopted for interviews.
- Articles written in journals by personnel managers and recruiters in personnel or industrial psychology.

Most professional companies' interview procedures and suggested improvements are often dealt with in detail in some of these journals. These include journals for the banks, police, medical professions, insurance companies and the teaching professions.

2.   Self-preparation Stage

The next section will help you to take steps to reduce the tension of the moment with mental preparation for every stage.

Self Examination

*   Identify your strengths and weaknesses. Make a list of them on paper and try to find positive points to offset your negative aspects. Interviewers often ask what your bad points are, so be prepared.
*   Visualise the interview situation.
*   Mentally review the surroundings and location of the interview.
*   Outline the steps you are going to take, from the time you knock at the door to the introduction, shaking hands with the interviewer, sitting down, looking at the interviewer, the type of posture you are going to adopt and, finally, leaving the room.
*   Prepare for the unexpected by thinking about what you are going to do if the telephone suddenly rings, if the interviewer drops a handkerchief, if a second interviewer is sitting behind your back or if the fire alarm goes off.
*   Review what you will say if invited to ask a question.

Hands-on Techniques

One of the most important insights of modern psychology is that we have got to be responsible for our own actions as much as possible if we want to lead positive and productive lives.

In the case of interview training we have got to internalise the behaviours which we know will impress the interviewer, i.e. we need to adopt the characteristics of the interviewer's ideal job applicant. These behaviours, which include verbal and non-verbal elements, have already been identified in this book. Therefore, all you need to do now is to make these your own. The hands-on techniques are specifically intended to do this.

In order to instil a very high level of confidence into yourself you have got to reflect on these techniques and develop potential situations for yourself that will adequately prepare you for the real thing.

In football and sporting terms, the overall approach that

internal practice involves has been referred to as 'psyching yourself up' for the task. It is vitally important that you carry out this process so that you will be able to give the interview your best shot. Situations and scenarios for your internalisation process are suggested in simulation exercises given below. You should use all the hands-on techniques in conjunction with such exercises.

Suggested simulations for you to work through are given below so you can visualise how it feels to be in the given situation and rehearse what you might do.

> *You are being interviewed for a bank. When you arrive at the bank you are met by the porter whom you think gruffly asks you what you want. You are shown to the room where the interview is to take place. You knock hesitatingly at the door and you are asked to come in. The room is a small reception room attached to the bank. There are pictures of former bank managers all around the room, as well as some works of art. The atmosphere is rather cold and impersonal. The interviewer has spectacles and is dressed in grey. He looks at you over his spectacles and begins to interview.*

If you stumble into this kind of situation without internal preparation, you may perform very badly indeed, whereas if you try to visualise how you are going to act, you should be able to adjust yourself to it rapidly. We have been told that man is the most adaptable living being on this planet. You must remember this and adapt yourself to whatever situation presents itself.

> *You have applied for a job with an engineering firm. When you arrive at the premises five minutes before the appointment, you are met by the secretary who invites you into the reception room. The interviewer, who is one of the managers, arrives and begins to show the work that the company does. You are shown maps of the local harbour and told that the firm is engaged in drilling operations. Another employee comes in and begins to show you how the computer systems works, no one asks you any questions for a long time. You begin to feel very ill at ease and a cold sweat breaks out through you. Finally, after about one hour of touring around the plant the interviewer says, "Well, tell me about yourself."*

This is an unusual situation and you have got to anticipate it. It is very disconcerting not to be asked any questions at all when you have come to the interview with a great deal of preparation done and you find that no one wants to know about it. Visualising in advance is the best way to help to cope with this predicament.

Role-playing Exercises

In the case of the two interviews above you should try to adopt the roles of the interviewers. In the first case, you have to imagine how busy and, possibly, harassed the 40 year old banker is likely to be. You have to compose the types of questions that he is likely to ask You have to decide whether there is going to be a preponderance of one type of question over the other so you can get a feel for the direction of the interview (see Chapters 4, 5 and 6).

Every interviewer has an outlook on life and you have to think about what it is likely to be. Is he a golfer or a family man with his own cares? Is she highly or moderately educated, interested in economic matters or in swimming? What is her physical appearance? Is he fit and trim or somewhat overweight?

Observe what kind of non-verbal communication signals he/she is giving so that you can be on your guard when trying to gauge the reaction to your answers.

You have to think of other matters which have been referred to in this book such as company ethos, selection policy (Chapter 6) and the likely philosophic approach to life of the interviewer.

Busy managers are unlikely to show you around their premises without having a specific purpose related to the interview in mind and you have got to think about what such an approach might be intended to achieve. The company may simply be conducting a public relations exercise rather than needing employees at this time. On the other hand it may be that your ability to deal with stress is being tested.

The approach being adopted may be intended to test your initiative. You must be ready to make comments on aspects of the workings of the job in this type of interview. You are being afforded an opportunity through the interviewer's silence. If you ask questions about various procedures you can show your interest and enthusiasm, particularly if these questions are based on research you have done on the company.

Remember the variations in interview styles, locations and situations, which are quite extensive. Think your way through as many of these as possible in advance. If your role-playing exercises involve thinking your way into the interviewer's mind set, as well as adopting his/her occupational role, you will greatly enhance your ability to establish rapport. Even though you may feel that you don't know enough about the way the interviewer looks at things, you will benefit enormously from actively trying to understand different approaches to occupational selection.

Modelling Exercises

This technique refers to the process of modelling yourself on other people. Already, this book has given you a great deal of information and insight into the way matters are looked at in different employment circles. What you need to do, in the case of modelling, is to study the way people in your target career area perform. At its simplest level it can be merely a matter of dressing the way the particular employee does and, at its most complex, it refers to the thinking process. In the case of this technique, however, you have to be very careful not to model yourself on an idealised role of the career in question which is obtained from glamourised television serials. Thus, the models you obtain in the media of the policeman, doctor, lawyer, nurse or teacher may have very little relation to reality.

For good modelling to take place the following guidelines should be followed.

- The model should be unusual and distinct enough to make a lasting impression on you.
- You need to be highly motivated if you are to successfully acquire skills through modelling yourself on another person.
- You need to be able to observe the model in as many situations as possible.
- You need to understand the work environment of the person in question.
- The behaviour that you are trying to imitate will be more successfully internalised if it relates to something you know or have experienced already.

3.   Interactive Training Techniques

Training Approach

At this stage you will have to give particular attention to the highest level of authenticity in your DIY training programme.

Since the interview is a two-way process you have got to find some way of simulating it so that the training will reflect the real situation. You may be in a position to engage a professional interview trainer to do this work for you but, if you adopt this procedure you must ensure that you are getting value for money. In many ways a mother, father, husband, wife or a friend can be as good as a professional trainer, provided you take the appropriate precautions in order to ensure that a very high level of authenticity applies. The appropriate precautions in relation to the various components of the interactive stage are outlined under the guidelines given below.

•   Determine specific guidelines for your trainer.
•   Use the training techniques outlined above in interactive situations.
•   Ensure that at least one training interview takes place in an environment that reflects totally the real situation.

Since this is the third stage in a three-part training process, there should be a very natural progression in the learning curve. The training exercises that you will carry out at this stage will be similar to those which you carried out at the self-preparation stage except that, at the interactive stage, you are interacting with another person.

Guidelines for your 'Trainer'

•   Ensure that the 'trainer' has a copy of the CV which you sent in to the company.
•   If possible, provide the trainer with a copy of the interview guide which the company uses for selection.
•   Ask the trainer to read this book, particularly the sections that deal with different types of questions.
•   Provide the trainer with the documentation about the organisation which you have studied yourself.

- Make an audiotape or, preferably, a videotape of the interview and of the trainer's comments.
- Insist that the trainer follow the guidelines mentioned below for proper feedback.
- Tell the trainer to use all the different styles described in this book.

Characteristics of Good Feedback

- It is descriptive rather than evaluative.
- It is specific rather than general.
- It is directed towards behaviour that the receiver can control.
- It is requested rather than imposed.
- It is given immediately.

Use of Tape Recorders or Video Tape Recorders

The use of one or other of these pieces of equipment provides you with an unsurpassable way of training yourself in interview skills. Both provide you with the following benefits.

- A way of recording the words of people in the occupations you wish to enter.
- A way of recording your own responses to interview questions which can afterwards be evaluated by an expert in the field in question.
- An atmosphere of threat which effectively simulates the real interview situation.
- A mechanism which you can replay in order to discover whether your modelling behaviour is effective.
- A way through which you can evaluate your own performance.
- An insight into the strategies which others adopt when they feel threatened.

Despite the above benefits it is extremely important for you to realise that there are certain disadvantages about using such equipment in training. These include the following.

- There is tendency for trainers and trainees to focus on the means rather than the end and pose for the camera and get lost in the technique of recording the video.
- It can be off-putting for some people to hear their own voices or to see their own presentations and some confidence can be lost at first.
- Interview candidates who have had a lot of training through these methods can acquire a certain gloss which some interviewers don't like.

Guidelines for Effective Video and Audio Interview Training

There is no doubt that using a tape recorder and/or video recorder enhances performance when it is used by a trainer for the purpose of role playing, modelling, simulation and feedback exercises. In order to use these instruments most effectively for interview training the following guidelines should be observed.

Conduct a full scale analysis of your performance in a section by section way.

Tips for Interview Training

- Answers which you have given that don't seem to address the interviewer's questions should be isolated and corrected versions should be prepared by the trainer or by yourself.
- The various key concepts that have already been mentioned in this book should be highlighted.
- Both the trainer and the trainee should take notes regarding the areas where there appear to be weaknesses.
- Observe how you are able to develop other thoughts regarding various questions that you have been asked as soon as the analysis is finished.
- Identify the sections of the interview which were the key turning points.
- Clarify for yourself whether there were any blatant contradictions in your answers.
- Ask a number of people to comment on your performance but tell them to keep the guidelines for good feedback in mind when doing so.

- Record the trainer's and other commentators' remarks on the tape.
- Replay the interview a number of times before the real interview and try to absorb the comments of your evaluator.
- Make sure you take a constructively critical approach to your evaluators as well as yourself, remember they too can be wrong.

With the above approach to DIY interview training you will heighten your own awareness, your responsiveness to the underlying thrust of interviewers and your understanding of the overall context in which interviews take place.

No matter how much preparation you do, it is difficult to surpass the effectiveness of an interview in a real situation with a professional, from the area in which you are interested, conducting the interview. This type of training technique is the final technique that you ought to use some time before the important interview if you are to get maximum benefit from experience.

The Full-scale Simulated Interview

It is said that a simulation cannot be fully effective unless it has 'psychological fidelity' which means that it must reflect the real situation in every possible way. The outline given below will guide you in setting up an effective interview experience for yourself in which you can practice the skills which you have learned in this book.

Tips for Effective Interview Simulations

- Ask a professional (someone in business, your doctor or dentist) to interview you for an imagined position in his/her organisation.
- Have the interview conducted on the company premises
- Make an appointment for the interview through the company secretary.
- Send in your application form and CV.
- Ensure that there is an appropriate period of waiting outside the interviewer's office.
- Ask the interviewer to introduce some change during the

interview so that you will learn how to adjust in real situations.

- Ask the interviewer to make it as realistic as possible.
- Obtain permission to use a video or tape recorder to record the interview and the comments of the interviewer.
- Ask for objective feedback and record all comments.
- Try to get two people to conduct the interview, if possible, so that you will be dealing with a panel. Your trainer might help in this respect.
- Ask the interviewer to read the relevant sections of this book in order to ensure comprehensive treatment.

Debriefing Session

The above session must be followed by a debriefing session if you are to bring about improvements in your performance. Identify the various stages in the interview and try to understand which elements in the situation gave you most problems. In order to consolidate what you have learned from the DIY interview training programme, you should re-read this book and identify those areas which seem to fit in with what you, yourself, have learned from the hands-on experiences you had.

The DIY Approach to Aptitude Test Training

The overall approach to training in aptitude tests should be the same as the DIY training programme for the employment interview. Therefore there should be:

- a research stage;
- a self-preparation stage;
- an interactive stage.

The Research Stage

This stage is concerned with the following points.

- Identifying the principal aptitudes that people have by referring to the analysis in Chapter 8.
- Establishing what are your own weaknesses.
- Practising examples in your daily life as already indicated.
- Gathering the necessary materials such as training manuals for the job, a description from former job applicants of their tests and copies of the trade journals which contain

practical examples of concepts in which the company is likely to test you.

- Studying video material such as that available in Open University courses in order to get a good idea concerning the equipment that the company is using.
- Telephoning the company to see if they will tell you in which aptitudes precisely they are going to be testing you.

The Self-preparation Stage: A Step by Step Procedure

Step 1 Set yourself tests similar to those you find in reading material you have gathered during the research stage, e.g. by looking at pictures of the plant or equipment that the company uses you will be able to identify the kinds of concepts that are in daily use by company personnel.

Step 2 Study a set of verbal reasoning tests and discover the underlying principles that are being tested – a number of them have already been identified above.

Step 3 Identify your greatest weaknesses and focus on improving these areas.

Step 4 Study a set of numerical ability tests and follow the same procedure as in steps 2 and 3.

Step 5 Study a set of spatial tests and follow the same procedures as above.

Step 6 Do a complete test for each of the aptitudes and read the explanations regarding why you had incorrect answers.

Step 7 Mix the three aptitudes together in an orderly way – verbal, numerical and spatial analogues and, subsequently, in a varied fashion, i.e. verbal, numerical and spatial etc.

The Interactive Stage

At this stage you should have completed stages 1 and 2 above and you will either be conducting final preparations or you will be sitting in the examination hall doing the test.

Tips for Final Preparations

- Don't do vast numbers of aptitude tests the day before the actual session because you are likely to confuse rather than enlighten yourself.

- Review the tests mentioned in Chapter 8 and consult the answers when you are stuck.
- Look for the general underlying principles and patterns in the tests.
- Try to run your mind over all possible types with your eyes closed so that you can visualise the different alternatives with which you may be presented.
- Because of the intensive nature of aptitude testing sessions, you should have a good night's sleep before them. If you have to travel a long distance you should, if at all possible, arrive at the location the night before.

Tips for the Selection Testing Session

- Arrive well in advance of the time because the nervous tension which lateness will cause may reduce your performance considerably.
- Supervisors will usually give very explicit instructions regarding how the tests are to be done and make sure you pay full attention to these.
- Make sure you have an adequate supply of pens and pencils and make sure you mark the answer sheet in the exact way you are told – your answers may be corrected electronically and you will have been told to bring a certain type of pencil or pen with you.
- Always be certain that the section of the answer sheet you are using corresponds with the questions you are given – many marks are lost because students write their answers in the wrong grid.
- Before the test, calculate the time for each item carefully by dividing the total number of items into the time available.
- Remember that the easier items usually come at the beginning of the test and you should allow for this in estimating. Don't spend too long at any one test because you could find yourself running out of time very rapidly.
- Because of the intensity of sets of aptitude tests, you may find yourself tired after them and you should make provision for this, particularly if you have a series of tests as well as an

interview on the same day, which is often the case at the assessment centres.

- Remember, the tests have been compiled in such a way that there is only one correct answer in each case.
- While doing the tests remember your own preparation and think of the fundamental principles that are being tested.
- If you have prepared well you will be able to identify the items which you are best at – obviously you should go through these more rapidly than those in which you are weak.
- Remember, employment recruiters usually select the top 20-25 per cent at the screening stage – this means that you must have approximately 75-80 per cent of the items correct in order to be called for interview.
- Remember, also, that some companies will tell you how you performed in the aptitude tests and this will give you an excellent indication about what you should concentrate on for your next aptitude tests.

Conclusion

This book has outlined for you how you can be successful in aptitude tests and at interviews. It has identified key concepts and has pointed out how you, yourself, can determine, to a large extent, the direction which an interview takes. The usual criteria under which interviewers evaluate job applicants have been referred to – the pitfalls, the types of questions you may be asked, the responses you ought to give and the philosophic principles underlying company policy.

You have been given suggestions regarding the data you need to accumulate and where you are likely to find it in order to impress the interviewers.

You may use a professional trainer to bring you through all of the procedures and situations that have been outlined or you may use people around you to help. No matter which of these courses of action you adopt, the most fundamental feature in all of the preparatory exercises that you undertake is that you have the star role. It is your motivation, your preparatory work, your interview skills, your aptitude strengths, your track record, your coping skills, your confidence and your ability to market yourself that has got to come through. It simply can't come through if you don't prepare. After all, you prepare for every other examination and spend hours practising the skills which help you to survive and succeed.

One of the most difficult survival tasks facing people in modern times is that of finding and obtaining work. Therefore, you should prepare well for this hurdle if you want to be successful. You should re-read this book many times and, above all, you should practise your skills as often as possible in real situations.

Dogged persistence coupled with realistic interview experiences, as well as adequate and complete self-evaluation will help you to achieve a successful outcome.

Appendix

The Professional Interview Skills Trainer

In modern times we have become accustomed to hiring professionals to carry out various activities for which we feel we have no competence ourselves. At the practical level of everyday activities specialisations have arisen for dealing with many areas, such as window cleaning, varnishing, curtain hanging, interior decoration and carpet laying. There are also new fields of expertise in intellectual pursuits such as carbon dating in archeology or computer-assisted, qualitative analysis in the social sciences. A cursory glance at a bibliography of topics in any of the sciences gives us an awesome outline of the range of topics which are considered to be specialisations in their own right.

Many such specialisations have grown in answer to perceived gaps in services. We don't question anymore the need for such a focus on matters that are considered to be of importance in contemporary society. We are satisfied once we conclude that the people providing the expertise know what they are talking about and are able to get central tenets across to us in coherent manner or are able to perform effectively when we require work to be done.

In the field of interview skills also there are cogent arguments for hiring the services of a professional trainer to get the job done in the most effective way. These arguments can be summarised as follows.

- You can be pointed in the right direction in relation to the job area for which you are applying.
- You will be given feedback from a professional concerning your interview performance.
- The professional will be able to tell you how to improve your performance.
- You will be told where to get the information that you seem to be lacking.
- The trainer will be able to give you a realistic simulation of the real situation.
- A fully qualified trainer will be in a position to train you in

the taking of aptitude tests, as well as how to gain the maximum impact from your CV.

But, how do professional trainers do their work? How do they train people in effective interview performance? Is there a particular approach to interview skills training that is more effective than others? Do we need to talk about aptitude tests, interests inventories and personality profiles in the context of interview skills training? Is it better for me to hire a trainer to carry out the work for me than to do it myself?

The short answer to all of these questions is that we have to ask the trainer what he or she thinks. If the answer implies that it is best to engage a professional trainer the reader may feel justified in saying that the trainer is following his or her own agenda, whereas if the answer implies the opposite the reader may feel that the trainer is merely being self-effacing. For this reason, it is probably best to allow the reader to make up his/her own mind by describing the services provided by a training organisation.

Therefore, for the purposes of this chapter, the manner in which professional training is conducted at Lankford Counselling and Guidance Bureau (71, Wilton Court, Cork, Ireland: Telephone (353 0) 21-341032) will be described. Through this approach the reader will be given a baseline through which he/she can compare other similar services that are on offer.

The activities undertaken by this bureau can be divided into four sections.

1.   Career assessment.
2.   CV preparation.
3.   Aptitude test preparation.
4.   Interview skills training.

Sample Career Assessment Report

The following sample report outlines the main components that are included in a professional career assessment. The assessment deals with an adult who is anxious to enter a business career but is not sure whether he has the necessary career profile.

Name and Address of Client	Professional Trainer
James Exemplar 17, Clarity Row, Cork, Ireland.	Dr Cormac Lankford, MA Psychol. LCGB, 71, Wilton Court, Cork, Ireland. Tel: (353 0) 21-341032 Fax: (353 0) 21-341032 E-mail: lankfordc@yahoo.com Web site: www.silk.ie/lgb

Introduction

The idea behind career assessment is to conduct an audit into where a person stands at any particular point in his or her career. We conduct an audit of our financial affairs, at least once a year, when we have to face the demands of the revenue authorities. We sometimes conduct an audit of our health when we are worried about how we feel or about some pain that has begun to bother us. Similarly, it makes sense for us to conduct an audit of where we stand in regard to our careers.

Career assessment at Lankford Counselling and Guidance Bureau entails just such an audit. Candidates who undergo the audit are asked to sit for the comprehensive set of differential aptitude tests which have already been described in this book. They include verbal reasoning, numerical ability, abstract reasoning, clerical speed and accuracy, mechanical reasoning, space relations, spellings and language usage. The idea behind giving you these tests is to identify those areas where you have the greatest talents so that you can direct your attention towards interviews and vacancies where such talents are required. It does not make much sense to apply for jobs in which you have no talents, particularly at a time when there is an abundance of vacancies in the market place.

Career interests (as discussed in Chapter 2 of this book) are identified and related to the aptitudes so that a comprehensive career profile is built up. Such interests cover mechanical, computational, scientific, persuasive, aesthetic, literary, musical, social service, clerical, practical and medical. Where necessary the client may be given a personality questionnaire in order to shed light on personality aspects that are relevant. As well as these tests, account has to be taken of a client's achievements, personality and motivation, so that a decision can be made about appropriate careers that should be identified.

When all of the tests and questionnaires have been completed the client makes an appointment with the assessor for the purpose of drawing together the implications. The client and the assessor come to agreed conclusions about the educational and career outlets that exists for the fulfillment of such talents, achievements, career interests and personality orientations.

The Report

Rationale for Careers Assessment Approach to Subject and Career Choice

The following career assessment approach to subject selection is based on the rationale that if the four significant aspects of career choice (i.e. aptitudes, career interests, achievements and personality) are taken into account when people are choosing their educational course or career, there is a greater likelihood that correct choices will be made. A detailed analysis is given of your aptitudes and you are asked to relate these findings to:
• the results that you have achieved in examinations;
• the interests that have been identified in the career interests inventory;
• the findings in regard to your personality profile.

From an examination of aptitudes and achievements a number of career profiles can emerge.

1. **Client A** is excellent in all of his aptitudes, excellent in all of his subjects but doesn't know what career path he wants to follow.

2. **Client B** is excellent in all of her aptitudes, poor in all of her subjects and he doesn't know what career path she intends to follow.

3. **Client C** is poor in all of his aptitudes, excellent in all of his subjects and doesn't know the career path he intends to follow.

When we come to consider career interests there are further variations of which the following are some examples.

1. **Client A** is excellent in all of her aptitudes, excellent in all of her subjects and shows a high level of interest in a number of specific categories in the career interests inventory.

2. **Client B** is excellent in all of his aptitudes, poor in all of his subjects but is rather vague about the career interests that he has.

3. **Client C** is poor in all of his aptitudes, excellent in all of his subjects and is pretty consistent about the career interests that he has.

Personality orientations are identified in a similar way and related to aptitudes, achievements and interests so that an exceedingly comprehensive profile is built up and the client can make realist decisions based on this profile. In your case, the following analysis indicates where your strengths lie, the level of interest you have in certain career areas and how your personality can impact on the situation.

Aptitudes

Verbal Reasoning

Your score for verbal reasoning lies between the 70th and the 79th percentile ranking (i.e. where you stand in a typical group of 100 people of your age and range). It would, therefore, appear that you have a reasonable level of aptitude for careers in which a high level of verbal aptitude is required.

It would be incorrect to conclude that your score is extremely high, because quite a number of students in second level and third level colleges do well in this aptitude. It is regarded as an indication that you have a fairly good ability to reason logically in verbal terms.

However, the score is not sufficiently high for you to draw the conclusion that you should be able to cope with all higher level subjects. More information is needed concerning your ability for abstract thought before such a conclusion could be drawn. Verbal reasoning has to do with logical reasoning which is very important for many career areas.

This aptitude is relevant for people who wish to follow courses that lead to management positions. It is also important for people who follow courses in psychology, law and human resource management. To be able to think clearly and logically and to be able to bring all the data together before coming to a conclusion is quite an important aptitude for people who are in varied management working environments. Your score would suggest that you should have no trouble with essays or third level course areas where a high level of speculative thought is required.

> *Courses and career areas such as sales, marketing, finance and insurance need a fairly high level of verbal reasoning, if a student is to profit from them. You have such a high level of reasoning ability that you should not have difficulty in coping with such courses and careers, provided you apply yourself fully to the fundamental principles and practices associated with these vocational fields.*

Numerical Ability

Scores that lie between the 90th and 99th percentile ranking in numerical ability demonstrate very clearly that you have an extremely high level of aptitude for subjects and careers with a numerical bias. Numerical ability does not, of course, refer to higher level mathematics at all and no conclusions with respect to this subject can confidently be drawn on the basis of performance in numerical ability.

Even though computers and calculators have removed much of the drudgery associated with calculations, it is clear that such an aptitude is very helpful when dealing with subjects such as economics, accounting and, possibly, business organisation. Therefore, you should give careful consideration to the question of entering career areas where these subjects are important.

> *Courses and career areas where numerical ability is important include banking, finance, accounting, buying and selling or costing and estimating. It is also valuable in general business negotiations where an ability to calculate percentages, profit margins, reductions, taxes and overheads is vital.*

Abstract Reasoning

Students who achieve scores over the 80th percentile ranking in abstract reasoning show an extremely high level of ability in this aptitude and should have the capacity to follow courses leading to career options in architecture, design, draughting and certain kinds of computerisation. Furthermore, the subjects that are related to architecture, design and CAD (computer-aided design) are fairly specific so that if you know you have an aptitude for them you ought to have confidence in your ability for this occupational sector. Third level colleges dealing with these fields of activity like potential students to have good grades in art or technical drawing, higher mathematics and, frequently, foreign languages.

This test is the closest test in the battery of aptitude tests to a raw test of intelligence. Since the completion of the series is also involved it may be a case that the kind of aptitude involved in this test has to do with entrepreneurial ability.

You are given a certain series of shapes and you are asked to complete the series in a logical way. That is the kind of aptitude that people, need to a very high degree, when making decisions. It is one that is particularly useful when dealing with computerisation because it enables a person to reason abstractly without the use of words. Your score, which is over the 80th percentile ranking, demonstrates that you have a particularly high level of ability in this area.

Clerical Speed and Accuracy

Scores over the 90th percentile ranking in clerical speed and accuracy are rather high and they demonstrate that you are highly clerical, speedy and accurate in transferring data from one place to another. The score does not tell us anything at all about your level of intelligence but, generally speaking, the test is regarded as a good measure of aptitude for wordprocessing and clerical work.

Also in the case of accounting, it is necessary to be clerically orientated, to a certain extent, if you wish to perform well. For obvious reasons, it is vital to be a good, neat, accurate worker in banking positions because a lot of counting and entering of data is involved. Of course, it can be said that the work that was formerly carried out on typewriters is now carried out on the computer. This does not mean that the operator does not make errors. In fact, it must be stressed that mistakes are being made all the time at the data-entry stage. You have got to keep the dictum of computer gurus "garbage in garbage out" in mind when talking about the accuracy of the computer. It is clear from your score in this aptitude that you are very exact about transferring data and that you are likely to be excellent as a computer operator.

Mechanical Reasoning

Scores that lie between the 0 and 49th MR (mechanical reasoning) percentile ranking are very poor because students tend to achieve a very high mark in this aptitude.

Training bodies often give a mechanical reasoning test as part of the selection process. The cut off point is usually close to the 80th percentile ranking. Therefore, it would be very unwise of you to pursue courses in the mechanical field and if you are thinking of taking physics or technologically orientated subjects or courses you would first want to consider well what you are doing. Indeed, with this level of aptitude in mechanical reasoning you would need to think about ruling out careers with very high level technological concepts.

Space Relations

A score that lies between the 70th and 79th percentile rankings in this aptitude is well above average and it demonstrates that you have a very high level of competence in the area of space relations.

Since the score has to do with careers and subject areas such as physics, engineering, construction, higher level mathematics and technical drawing it is likely that you ought to be able to perform well in such fields of endeavour.

Due to the fact that technological careers require high levels of academic performance, as well as aptitude, you should not make decisions on the basis of the aptitude test result only.

Spelling

A score that lies in the 70th to 79th percentile ranking band is rather average and you would want to pay particular attention to this area. It is important to read carefully through all letters that you send out to employers or other personnel. You would want to ensure that your scores in this area are kept up to a certain standard. After all, if you were to look at this score in an objective way, it could be said that you had between 20-30 per cent of the most common words in the English language spelt incorrectly. A spelling test is often given by insurance companies when they are recruiting people for positions.

Language Usage

Scores that lie between the 1st and 49th percentile rankings are very poor and you should carefully consider the remaining options that are open to you in the educational sense. Students who achieve a score as low as this could find a great deal of difficulty in following courses at third level.

It should be said, however, that you can improve your scores in this aptitude if you pay more attention to grammar and expression. If you are sitting for sets of aptitude tests you would need to be extremely careful of language usage tests, because they are considered to be an indication of your level of educational attainment. Poor performance in them reflects badly on your level of education. You should remember that this is one of the tests where it is easiest to improve on the aptitude in question. Therefore, you need to look at the test again to see if you can identify the areas where you have the greatest weakness.

Career Interests

According to researchers, the career interests which we have remain relatively stable after the age of 17. A number of research projects have shown that if you measure a person's career interests at 17 and 35 there will be little change. Therefore, if a person's career interests are identified, they can give us a fairly good indication of the career category which is most appropriate for them.

In the context of assessment, of course, what is being referred to is inventoried interests. That is to say, the categories in question are based on the career interests that you indicate from a certain range of interests. In the case of the inventory that was used in this assessment there are 108 careers in all and these are divided initially into 9 divisions and, subsequently, into 12 different categories, which are outdoor, mechanical, computational, scientific, persuasive, aesthetic, literary, musical, social service, clerical, practical and medical.

You will appreciate that such categories represent a very wide variety of careers. You were asked to rate your choices in each division from 1 to 12 and by totalling the scores it is possible to arrive at what your 1st, 2nd, 3rd, 4th, 5th, 6th, 7th, 8th, 9th, 10th, 11th and 12th categories were. In the case of such totals researchers have concluded that when any total is less than 25 it shows a very strongly preferred category. In other words such a total will contain many examples of first, second and third choices.

This inventory is also divided up into two sections: a forced choice section and a free choice section. In the case of the forced choice section you were forced into making choices by being asked to rate from 1st to 12th as indicated above. These ratings are then divided into the categories mentioned above. At the bottom of the inventory you were asked to make free choices where you could put down any careers you liked. This is a very useful approach to career interests because it enables you and your counsellor to see if your forced and free choices are in the same category. If they are you can then have greater confidence in the findings, but if they aren't you may need to think about the matter further.

Consistency in the First Three Forced Choices

In order to get a close-up view of categories in which you are most interested, it makes sense to look at your first three choices. If these come to less than 84 they will show that you have a fairly strong preference for these three career areas. Of course, you need to look more closely at them in order to find out which of them are under 25. However, certain combinations of career

interests will indicate whether there is a high level of consistency between your first three categories or not. Some of these combinations are as follows.
1.   Computation, persuasive, social service.
2.   Medical, social service, persuasive.
3.   Mechanical, practical, persuasive.
4.   Musical, literary, aesthetic.
5.   Clerical, computational, practical.

There are a number of other combinations that make sense which are not included here. These matters are normally teased out between the counsellor and the client in the discussion that takes place.

Some combinations that are rather inconsistent are the following.
1.   Medical, mechanical, outdoor.
2.   Literary, scientific, mechanical.

However, we have to be very careful about such matters because a great deal may depend on the attitude of the student. In the broad, general sense it is possible to draw conclusions on the basis of the above analysis of career interests. For example, in the first case at the top of this page (computation, persuasive, social service) you can say that the student may have an interest in careers such as accountancy, provided that opportunities are available for dealing with people and managing projects of various kinds. Furthermore, accountancy may enable a client to satisfy his/her basic need for interaction with people that comes, in the first instance, from an interest in social service activities.

In the second case (medical, social service, persuasive) the field of medicine may refer to a student becoming a doctor, while at the same time being engaged in practical activities that will relate to running hospitals and organising various matters for others. In regard to the persuasive element this may be satisfied by being able to do some lecturing in medical matters which is an activity that many doctors involve themselves in as an integral part of their careers.

The third example given above (mechanical, practical, persuasive) is relatively straightforward because what is being referred to is engineering or technological careers with a management bias. Of course, most careers have a management component today.

The fourth category (musical, literary, aesthetic) is often one that refers to a certain type of individual who will show a strong leaning towards aesthetic in aptitude tests.

The fifth one (clerical, computational, practical) also is very close to the actual skills that a person will need to have if he/she hopes to be successful in accountancy, financial or, indeed, various practical career fields.

Your Career Interests

In your case the first three choices are computational, clerical and outdoor. This is the case with the forced choice section of the questionnaire. There is a very high level of consistency between number 2 and 3 indicating that you have a strong preference for these fields. Furthermore, your total for each of these categories comes to less than 25 which indicates that you have a very strong preference for such categories. In other words, you have given more ones, twos and threes for careers in these categories.

When you take these findings in conjunction with the findings in relation to aptitudes the picture that emerges is of someone who has real strengths in the computational and clerical fields.

Of course, it does not necessarily follow from this that you are going to achieve very high performance in such areas. It is rather a case of you having the basic strengths of practitioners in such fields. There are many other factors, such as motivation, level of attention, tuition and other considerations, which relate to performance.

Achievements

Candidly, it does seem that your achievements do not reflect your aptitudes to any great extent. As recommended to you during the consultation, it would appear that you ought to have achieved higher grades in your senior level examinations in business subjects such as economics and accountancy. Your score in verbal reasoning implies that you ought to have achieved fairly a high score in economics, whereas the numerical ability score would suggest that accountancy should present no great problems. We talked at some length about the certified public accountancy course which you have pursued and your disappointment at not achieving a better result in your examinations.

You informed me that you had spent two weeks studying each subject and that you were sometimes distracted when it came to settling down to study. This length of time is hardly sufficient for someone who wishes to do well in certified public accounting examinations. The failure rate is rather high in this examination and since this is the case you would need to focus a great deal more on the programme of studies. You should have a close look at your study habits

There are three key elements in learning. These are: initial learning, retention and recall. From what you said yourself it appears that you are learning the material reasonably well and that you have the ability to retain it. Your great problem seems to be in the area of recalling the material at examination time. As was suggested to you, the best way of bringing about improvement in this area would appear to be through learning some positive study techniques. You need some systematic way of organising the knowledge in your head so that when it comes to examination time you will be able to recall the material easily. In the consultation some suggestions were made about memory maps and spatial techniques that can be helpful in this regard.

Should you wish to discuss these matters further you can make another appointment. However, before you do this it would be beneficial for you to learn as much of the material as you can first. In relation to accountancy it might be useful to identify for yourself all the potential pitfalls in the examination papers and then, subsequently, find some way of classifying in your head appropriate ways of dealing with these questions.

Personality Orientations and Patterns

From the questionnaires you were given on your personality orientation and your level of motivation, it can be seen that you have an orientation towards factual areas and that you like to have fairly clear answers to questions that you have. It also seems that you wish to be working in a group situation rather than on your own and that you consider your personality to be fairly assertive. Concerning the matter of motivation, I can see from questionnaire that you have an interest in executive-type careers where you will have the opportunity of making decisions.

Conclusions and Recommendations

In conclusion then it can be said that you have fairly high aptitudes for areas of study concerned with computational types of
careers. These careers can be considered to cover a very broad
area that would include: accounting, clerical work, computer
work, secretarial work, finance, insurance or purchasing and
materials management. We discussed the area of purchasing
and materials management at some length and I think that this
is an area you might consider for the following reasons.

- You have the aptitudes and the career interests for good performance in this field of activity.
- The examinations of the Institute of Purchasing and Materials Management may not be quite as difficult for you as the
  accountancy examinations.
- You may get exemptions from certain sections of the Institute of Purchasing and Materials management examinations.
- Your personality orientation and job motivation appear to be
  in the direction for working with a group which is dealing
  with factual areas and which has to make group decisions in
  relation to its work.

Other possibilities that we talked about referred to marketing or
sales but I think that these areas would not be as beneficial for
you as the ones mentioned above.

Readers can see that the above profile gives the client a very
clear idea of her own strengths and weakness in relation to a
career in the field of accounting. Obviously, it would be better
for this client to apply for a position within an accounting environment than any other type of environment. Furthermore, it is
very evident that the type of exercise that has been conducted
above is the *sine qua non* for successful performance in an interview. Similar assessments to the above example are conducted
at LCGB in relation to all career areas. Strictly speaking all interview candidates should undertake a similar type of assessment to that which is outlined above before they sit in front of
an interview panel.

Bringing about a high level of compatibility between your talents, your achievements, your interests and personality orientation for the purpose of obtaining a suitable position will enable you to convince the interview panel that you have the right characteristics for the position on offer.

2.   The Professional Trainer and the CV

At LCGB sessions are also conducted on intensive CV preparation. As well as the tips and hints that are given already in Chapter 9, the value of using a professional trainer has a great deal to do with the fact that you need to highlight areas in your CV that you may be asked about in the interview. This will mean that you need to refer to every single achievement that you have had throughout your life. Such achievements need to be related to key elements of the jobs for which you are applying. A professional trainer will be able to highlight the analogies that exist between your experiences and the requirements of the positions.

A professional trainer with a background in counselling will enable you to gain access to strengths which you never though you had.

The following vignettes illustrate how this can be achieved at Lankford Counselling and Guidance Bureau.

A client felt that he had no hobbies at all and didn't know what he should put down under this heading in his CV. After some discussion and a good deal of prodding, it transpired that he kept pigeons. It may appear that pigeons are not very relevant to a position as a draper's assistant and, of course, this is quite true. However, the fact that this client was able to talk fluently about his pigeons, their customs, the distance they travelled, the messages they took from place to place, as well as the skill of caring for them, enabled him to convince the interviewers that he was a committed person who could give detailed attention to whatever task he had in hands.

Through a professional consultation at Lankford Counselling and Guidance Bureau this expertise was highlighted in his CV in such a way that the interviewers were prompted to ask questions about the matter.

A more striking example is one that concerns a client's ability to win championship games at chess.

> *The trainer couldn't play chess but he knew that chess players have a great grasp of mathematical concepts. The client in question had not achieved a very good result in his accountancy examinations, even though he excelled at chess. When preparing the CV the fact that he was a competent chess player and that he had won major distinction in the game was highlighted. Subsequently, he attended an interview and managed to obtain a position as a trainee accountant. He has long since qualified in the area.*

3. The Professional Trainer and Aptitude Test Preparation

In this field the expertise of the professional trainer lies in his ability to identify your weaknesses very rapidly, to set you tasks in those areas where you have greatest difficulty and, above all, to afford you the opportunity of practising as many examples as possible in a controlled situation. This is the approach adopted at Lankford Counselling and Guidance Bureau. It means that clients can spend a full week engaged in preparing for their aptitude tests. A good deal of time needs to be spent identifying all the different types of questions that you can get in the screening test for a job.

Success has a great deal to do with identifying the principles that are involved in each individual test so that you can address your mind to the ones that are giving you most difficulty.

After identifying the areas of weakness, the professional trainer at LCGB will spend an intensive period of time drilling you in the best way to deal with such areas.

4. The Professional Trainer and Interview Skills

Preparation

The interview skills preparation programme at LCGB adopts a psychological model that provides for the following five dimensions.

1. A simulated interview with the client by the professional trainer in which open, closed, primary and secondary questions are used.
2. An analysis of the client's level of interview skills preparedness through a review of the videotaped simulated interview.
3. A gut reaction from the interview trainer that is similar to the reaction of an interview panel in the first five minutes of an interview.
4. An extensive review of the simulated interview plus detailed feedback.
5. Detailed information on the position being applied for coupled with sample answers to the questions asked.

All trainer comments are recorded on the videotape so that the client has detailed comments on all aspects of his or her interview skills. The client then studies the tape and listens to the comments until such time as he or she has acquired the ability to deal with the different types of questions that are asked. The videotaped comments provide the client with a framework within which improvements can be brought about so that the client will have a positive image about themselves as they approaches the crucial test.

Bibliography

K Abercrombre, "Paralangue" *British Journal of Discourse Communication* (1968) Vol. 3, 55-59.

I R Andrews & Valenzi, "Individual Differences in the Decision Process of Employment Interviewers" *Journal of Applied Psychology* (1973) 54.

R D Arvey & J E Campion, "The Employment Interview, a Summary and Review of Recent Research" *Personnel Psychology* (1982) 35, 281-322.

R D Arvey, "Unfair Discrimination in the Employment Interview: Legal and Psychological Aspects" *Psychological Bulletin* (1979) Vol. 86, 4, 736-765.

M Argyle, *The Psychology of Interpersonal Behaviour* (London: Penguin Books) 1972.

R J Babcock & J C Yeager, "Coaching for the Interview: Does it Change Students into Puppets?" *Journal of College Placement* (1973) 33, 61-64.

J R Barbee et al, "Techniques of Job Interview Training for the Disadvantaged: Videotape Feedback, Behaviour Modification and Micro Counselling" *Journal of Applied Psychology* (1973) 58, 209-213.

S A Beebe, "Eye Contact, a Non-verbal Determinant of Speaker Credibility" *Speech Teacher* (1974) 23, 21-25.

J O Bolster & B M Springbett, "The Reactions of Interviewers to Favourable and Unfavourable Information" *Journal of Applied Psychology* (1961) 45, 96-103.

J O Britton & K R Thomas, "Age and Sex as Employment Variables, Views of Employment Service Interviewers" *Journal of Employment of Counselling* (1973) 18, 186-188

E Butler & M Pirie, *Boost Your IQ* (London: Pan Books Ltd) 1990.

Caroll, Pain and Ivancevich, "The Relative Effectiveness of Training Methods: Expert Opinion and Research" *Personnel Psychology* (1972) 5, 8-17.

R E Carlson et al, "The Effect of Interview Information in Altering Valid Impressions" *Journal of Applied Psychology* (1971) 54, 193-207.

M Cook & J M C Smith, "The Role of Gaze in Impression Formation" *British Journal of Social and Clinical Psychology* (1975) 14, 19-25.

H L Dipboye et al, "Relative Importance of Applicant Sex, Attractiveness and Scholastic Standing in Evaluation of Applicant Resumes" *Journal of Applied Psychology* (1975) Vol. 69, 1, 118-128.

G Duffy, "Giz a Job" Interview Training Programmes (Dublin: Bank of Ireland) 1988.

A G Eliott, "Study of Interview Procedures in the Bank of Ireland Trinity College, Dublin" *Journal of Occupational Psychology* (1981) 54, 265-273

H J E Eysenck, *Know Your Own IQ* (London: Penguin Books) 1990.

H J E Eysenck, *Check Your Own IQ* (London: Penguin Books Ltd) 1966.

C Fletcher, *Get That Job* (London, Harper Collins) 1992.

J P Galassi et al, (1978) "Preparing Individuals for Job Interviews: Suggestions From More Than 60 Years of Research" *Personnel and Guidance Journal* (1978) 57, 188-191.

Grifitt & Jackson, "Influence of Information About Applicant Ability and Non-ability on Personnel Selection Decisions" *Psychological Reports* (1970) 27, 144-156.

J A Hall, "Voice Tone and Persuasion" *Journal of Personality and Social Psychology* (1980) 38, 924-934.

Hakel & Schuh, "Job Applicant Attributes Judged Important Across Seven Divergent Occupations" *Personnel Psychology* (1971) 24, 45-52.

J G Hollandsworth et al, "Relative Contributions of Verbal, Articulative and Non-verbal Communication to Employment Decisions in the Job Interview Setting" *Personnel Psychology* (1979) 32, 359-367.

Hamberg et al, "Preparing Unemployed Youth for Job Interviews: A Controlled Evaluation of Social Skills Training" *Behaviour Modification* (1982) 6, 299-322.

A Keenan, "Some Relationships Between Interviewers Personal Feelings About Candidates and Their General Evaluation of Them" *Journal of Occupational Psychology* (1977) 50, 272-283.

J A Langdale & J Weltz, "Estimating the Influence of Job Information on Interview Agreement" *Journal of Applied Pscyhology* (1973) 65, 501-506.

C Lankford, "The Effectiveness of Behavioural Approaches to Training in Interviewee Skills" (Department of Applied Psychology, University College, Cork, Ireland, unpublished MA thesis) 1985.

C V Lewis et al, "Interview Training: Finding the Facts and Minding the Feelings" *Personnel Management* (1976) 8, 29-33.

E V Mayfield et al, "Selection Interviewing in the Life Insurance Industry: An Update of Research and Practice" *Personnel Psychology* (1980) 33, 725-739.

H McGinley et al, "The Influence of a Communicator's Body Position on Opinion Change in Others" *Journal of Personality and Social Psychology* (1975) 31, 686-690.

T Prone, *Get That Job* (Dublin: Poolbeg Press) 1993.

C Roberts, *The Interview Game* (London: BBC) 1985.

M Rothlsstein & D N Jackson, "Decision Making in the Employment Interview: An Experimental Approach" *Journal of Applied Psychology* (1980) 65, 271.

J H Sterret, "The Job Interview: Body Language and Perceptions of Potential Effectiveness" *Journal of Applied Psychology* (1978) 63, 388-390.

D E Sutton & F O Carleton,"Students Rate the College Rectuiters" *Journal of College Placement* (October 1962).